David Philip Lindsley

The Note-Taker

Elements of tachygraphy

David Philip Lindsley

The Note-Taker
Elements of tachygraphy

ISBN/EAN: 9783337277345

Printed in Europe, USA, Canada, Australia, Japan

Cover: Foto ©Andreas Hilbeck / pixelio.de

More available books at **www.hansebooks.com**

NOTE-TAKER;

OR,

ELEMENTS OF TACHYGRAPHY,

PART II.

A TREATISE

ON

THE SECOND STYLE OF LINDSLEY'S BRIEF WRITING.

FOR THE USE OF

LAWYERS, EDITORS, REPORTERS, STUDENTS, AND ALL PERSONS DESIROUS OF TAKING FULL NOTES IN COURTS OF RECORD, PROFESSIONAL SCHOOLS AND SEMINARIES, AND PUBLIC ASSEMBLIES.

BY

DAVID PHILIP LINDSLEY.

BOSTON:
OTIS CLAPP & SON 3 BEACON STREET.
CHICAGO: D. KIMBALL, P. O. BOX 898.
1873.

Entered according to Act of Congress, in the year 1878, by
DAVID P. LINDSLEY,
in the Office of the Librarian of Congress, at Washington.

*Stereotyped by
Whitcomb & Co., Boston.*

DEDICATION.

To the Rev. SAMUEL H. WINKLEY,
                                    Boston:

Rev. and Dear Sir,
            Permit me in dedicating this work to one whose abundant labors for the little ones of Christ's flock deserve a better tribute to recall an incident in the introduction of the art in Boston.

Discouraged by the indifference of many whose aid and sympathy I had reason to expect, I appealed, as a last resort, to the entire clergy of the city. All who responded to the call deserve recognition here, and they represented the principal denominations of Christian people among us. Some of them have continued friends to the present time, and some have fallen asleep.

I desire to include in this memorial all who kindly appreciated and aided the art in that time of weakness.

Your Christian charity, through which I have learned much of the love of God, has been of inestimable service to me in keeping alive those sentiments of fraternal regard which unite men in sympathy, and perpetuate the arts of peace.

With the warmest sentiments of affectionate regard,

    I remain yours,

        In the cause of God and humanity,

            The AUTHOR.

PREFACE.

The nature of the style of writing taught in this work, the demand for it, and the degree of brevity and perspicuity gained in it, are discussed in the introductory pages. The persons for whom it is especially designed, and the style best adapted to each of the leading professions, may also be learned from the introductions to this and the previous volume.

It remains to give a few suggestions concerning the use of this work.

1. A previous knowledge of the ELEMENTS,—not merely a theoretical, but a practical knowledge,—is an essential foundation for rapid success in the study of this style. It is a mistake on the part of those who think that the practice of the longer forms given in the preceding volume is time and labor misdirected. Such practice is the quickest road to success in the briefer styles of the art. Long word-forms occur in the most contracted styles; and if the student shirks the labor of mastering them, he need never hope to become a swift writer. Those pupils invariably succeed best, and in the shortest time, who apply themselves diligently to the practice of the Elements until they can write seventy-five to ninety words a minute; then they are prepared to commence the NOTE-TAKER'S style.

2. The chapters of the present work should be studied and mastered consecutively; and each writing exercise

should be written in its order, corrected, and rewritten until the principles embodied in it are made practically useful.

3. The correction of the writing exercises by a competent teacher is the only way in which most persons will be likely to acquire a good knowledge of the style; but if any one is obliged to rely upon himself, by a diligent study of the illustrations and reading lessons, and a frequent revision of his own exercises, he may acquire skill and a fair degree of accuracy.

4. It is better to avoid writing miscellaneous exercises until those here given are mastered; but, if any one prefers to master a part of the book, and apply the principles first introduced without completing the style, it will do no injury. The work contains more contractions than are needed by all; but if a mode of contraction is introduced into a person's writing, it should be used intelligently. The habit of wresting a principle from its proper application, and applying it at random, as has been done so generally by amateur phonographers, is destructive to all excellence, and a source of confusion. The student should study one principle until that is mastered before advancing to the next principle.

With these suggestions to the student, and with thanks to all who have labored with us in the production of the work, we commend it to those whose labors it is designed to lighten.

ANDOVER, MASS., Sept. 3, 1873.

CONTENTS.

INTRODUCTION.

	Page.
The Measure of Success heretofore gained in the Introduction of Short-hand Writing	9
The Efforts made to this End	"
The Need of a Better System than the Old Phonography	10
A Style for Literary and Business Men	"
The Demand for a Style Adapted to Taking Notes, &c.	"
The Persons who need it	"
Its Use in Schools of a High Grade	11
Qualities of the Style demanded	12
Causes of the Failure of Phonography; its Indefiniteness	"
This Difficulty Avoided in Tachygraphy	"
Redundancy of Phonography	13
Numerous Signs for Single Letters	"
Various Modes of Combining Characters	"
The Letter *P*, with some of its Adjuncts in Phonography	14
The Letters *s t r d* Combined into Twenty Differing Outlines	15
The Labor of Acquiring the Phonographic Orthography	16
One Hundred and Twenty Thousand Word and Phrase Forms	"
The Upper Stories of the Phonographic Temple	17
Minute Distinctions	"
The Contractions used in Tachygraphy	18
Degrees of Complexity	"
Pure Phonic Signs	19
External Uniformity not Sufficient	20
FIRST RESULT	21
THE CONTRACTIONS OF THE NOTE-TAKER'S STYLE	"
Words of Frequent Occurrence Abbreviated	"
Phrase-signs	22
Compound Words of Latin and Greek Origin	"
Consonants Combined in Saxon Words	23

CONTENTS.

	Page.
Contractions Restricted in their Use	24
Average Rate of Public speaking	25
The REPORTING STYLE	26
M. Gourard in regard to Complexity of Outline	27
Acknowledgment of Services of Writers of Old School	28

CHAPTER I.

SHORTENED WORD-FORMS. 29

	Sect.
Word-Signs—their Classification	2
Table of Word-Signs	5
Explanation of the Table	6
Writing Exercise First 36	

CHAPTER II.

THE CIRCLE AND THE DOUBLE CIRCLE. 37

The Use of the Circle	10
Words of only Two Consonant Letters	11
Group of Words containing *l s*	12
Groups containing *r s*, *m s*, and *p s*	12
General Rule for the Use of the Circle	13
The Use of the Circle in Long Words	13—Rems.
The Circle for *z*	14
The Double Circle	15
S before Compounds of the *R* Series	16
The Circle before ⁄, ⁄, and ⁄	17
S before the Compounds of the *L*-Series, and ⌒ and ⌒	18
Vocalization of Words containing the Circle and Double Circle	19
Writing Exercise Second 55	
Writing Exercise Third 56	

CHAPTER III.

THE USE OF COMPOUND SIGNS. 59

Compounds of the *L* and *R* Series	21
The Use of *zher* and *sher* for *jer* and *cher*	22
The Use of *zhel* and *shel*, or *zhe-la* and *she-la*, for *jel* and *chel*	23
Writing Exercise Fourth 65	

CONTENTS. 5

	Sect.
The Prefixes *ab, ap,* &c. omitted	24
The Prefix *ad* before *v* and *j*	25
Writing Exercise Fifth	
Briefer Signs for Gua and Qua	26
Contracted Signs for Ha and Wha	28
Writing Exercise Sixth	

CHAPTER IV.

HALF-LENGTH CHARACTERS.

	Sect.
General Principles of Shortening	30
The Liquids Halved, — Heavy and Light	32
Ing and other Letters not Shortened	33
Angles Essential to the Use of Shortened Letters	35
The Shortened Letters not Used in *sound, hasty,* &c.	36
Shortened Letters used in *article, practical,* &c.	38
Est and *ste* Contrasted	39
Sest and *Sus-te* contrasted	40
Exceptional Forms	41
Writing Exercise Seventh	
Writing Exercise Eighth	

CHAPTER V.

LENGTHENED CURVES.

	Sect.
Double-Length Curves	42
The Liquid Curves	44
Vocalization of Lengthened Curves	45
Dr and *tr* followed by a Vowel	46
The Shortened ⌒, the Circle, and the Lengthened ⌒	48
Angles with Lengthened Curves	49
En and *ing* Trebled	50
Writing Exercise Ninth	
Writing Exercise Tenth	

CHAPTER VI.

PREFIXES. **101**

	Sect.
Composite Words	52
Simple Prefix Signs	54

CONTENTS.

	Sect.
Explanation of their use	55
Con and *Com*	55
Con and *Com* Radical	57
Writing Exercise Eleventh	
Contra	58
In and *Im*	59
Not used in certain cases	60
In and *Im* before the Circle	61
Intra, Intro, &c.	64
Magna and *Magni*	65
Self, With, Trans	66
Writing Exercise Twelfth	
Compound Prefixes	67
Circum	69
Writing Exercise Thirteenth	
Writing Exercise Fourteenth	

CHAPTER VII.

AFFIXES.

	Sect.
Table of Affix Signs	72
Specifications:—	
ment, mental, mentary	73
cient, tient, &c	74
sorcer	75
self and *with*	76
ward, ure	77
ural, urally, ual, and *ually*	79
uation and *ulation*	81
tional and *sional*	82
fication	83
The *shn* Hook	84
ation, otion, and *ution*	85
Writing Exercise Fifteenth	
Writing Exercise Sixteenth	

CONTENTS.

CHAPTER VIII.

MISCELLANEOUS CONTRACTIONS.   **137**

                                                                                                 Page.   Sect.

	Page	Sect
The Stems of Ha and Wha thickened		86
Thickened Ra, and the N-Hook		87
The Final Syllables *ance* and *ence*		88
The V and F-Hook		89
Derivative Word-Signs		90
The Plural of Nouns, and Third Singular of Verbs		90—1
The Termination *able*		90—2
The Terminations *ly, ed, ing, less, ic,* &c.		90—3 to 7
Contracted Words		91
Compound Words		92
Writing Exercise Seventeenth	.143	
Writing Exercise Eighteenth	.145	

CHAPTER IX.

PHRASE-SIGNS.   **147**

	Page	Sect
General Principles		93
The Signs for *in, have, all, of, the, us, they, though, may, are, will*		94
Sign for *ye* and *you*		95
The Tick for *he*		96
The Word *as* in certain Phrases		97
Lengthened Curves implying *there* and *their*		98
Shortened Phrases,—Contracted Sign for *at*, and the Omission of *and* and *the*		99
Can, for, from, has, I, it, not, &c. in Phrases		100
The Words *at, in, out,* &c. in Phrases		101
List of Words most used in Phrases		102—c
Simple Phrase-Signs,—Table A	.158	
Brief Phrase-Signs,—Table B	.159	
Special Phrases,—Table C	.160	
Tables D and E	.161-2	
Writing Exercise Nineteenth	.163	
Writing Exercise Twentieth	.165	

CHAPTER X.

THE TACHYGRAPHIC NOMENCLATURE. 167

	Sect.
Names of the Letters	102
Names of the Compounds of the L, R, and S-Series	103
The Double Circle, Halved Signs, &c.	104
Vocals and Vocal Hooks	105
Examples in Spelling	107
Names of Compound Signs,—Tables 171-2	
Writing Exercise Twenty-First 173	

CHAPTER XI.

ANALOGY AND EUGRAPHY. 175

	Sect.
Definition of the Word *Analogy*	109
The Laws of Analogy	110
Operation of the Laws of Analogy	111
Definition of the Word *Eugraphy*	112
The Principles of Eugraphy applied to Letters	113
Applied to Words and Phrases	115
The Requirements of Speed	116
The Brevity of Outlines	117
The Facileness of Outlines	118
The Nature of the Angles	119
Acute and Obtuse Angles	120
The Homogeneousness of the Curves	121
The Direction of the Curves influenced by Vocals	122
Outlines easily joined in Phrases	123
The Lineality of Outlines	124
The Requirements of Legibility	125
Consistency of Outline, &c.	126-8
The Use of Vocalization	129
Regard to the Relations of Words in Sentences	130
Conclusion	131
Writing Exercises Twenty-Second to Twenty-Fourth .197	
Vocabulary 223	

INTRODUCTION.

"IT WOULD BE MADNESS AND INCONSISTENCY TO SUPPOSE THAT THINGS WHICH HAV NEVER YET BEEN PERFORMED CAN BE PERFORMED WITHOUT EMPLOYING SOME HITHERTO UNTRIED MEANS." — *Lord Bacon in "Novum Organum."*

IN practical matters, theories and systems ar tested by experience, and succes gives proof of value. The mesure of succes gained in the introduction and actual use of short-hand writing in this country, up to the present time, is not very creditable to the means employed. We ar assured thro' varius channels that a large majority (some say three fourths) of the students in universities in Europe, especially in Germany, use brief writing in taking the lectures of their courses of study. In this country, not more than one student in fifty, in the schools of this grade, use short-hand in any form; and this, notwithstanding the immense labor of the Phonographers in their efforts to introduce that system.

Nor can it be said that this want of succes has been owing to any general indiference to the subject. Such has been the demand for works on Phonography that one publisher alone claims to have sold one hundred thousand (100,000) copies of a single text-book in this country; while those sold by others, and those imported from England, swell the amount to nearly or quite a quarter of a million copies. Had this sowing produced any reasonable harvest, we should hav had hundreds of thousands of writers of the art where we hav in reality only a few *hundreds*.

Besides this sale of books, teachers hav visited all schools of note in the country, and raised classes (or attempted to do so), and hav uniformly failed of any fair degree of succes in giving skill of writing in Phonography to their pupils; only one or two persons in classes numbering twenty or thirty students continuing the practice of the art, and fewer still gaining any great skill in its use.

With such facts before us, we trust that no further apology is needed for offering a system of brief writing better suited to the wants of the students of this country.

In the volume preceding this, "The Elements of Tachygraphy," we gave the elementary principles of a style adapted to the use of those literary and busines men who regard a high degree of legibility of more importance than a high rate of speed. We produced a style capable of being written from three to four times as rapidly as the common writing, while in perspicuity it equals the best of script. This style has been entirely succesful in its sphere — its simplicity and accuracy securing for it friends wherever it has been known. But the public mind has been led to regard the art as useful principally, if not entirely, for the taking of notes of public lectures, or for verbatim reporting, rather than as an aid in the study and the counting-room. This use of the art is certainly legitimate, and we provided, several years ago, a style peculiarly adapted to it. It was not convenient, nowever, to publish it at once; and, though taught by means of manuscripts, its publication has been delayed until the present time. We hav at last yielded to the solicitation of friends in all parts of the country, and offer this style, designed especially for NOTE-TAKING, to our friends and the public. The delay has not been entirely in vain, for it has enabled us to gradually perfect the style thro' its use during a number of years, and, with the final revision given it in preparing the following pages for the press, will, we hope, be found improved in simplicity and effectivnes.*

While the impresion that brief writing is of use mainly in the lecture or court room, or conference hall, is unfortunate, — since it must, we think, achieve its greatest succes as a substitute for the common writing, — yet there is a growing demand for more perfect reports of public assemblies; and the few well-trained reporters hav served principally as an example of what might be done in journalism were all our editors and reporters swift writers, and how

* For Key to spelling, see Rapid Writer. No. 11.

much the busines of our courts of record would be expedited by the use of brief and rapid writing by the lawyers and the court, as well as the profesional reporter. And in the lecture-room of the college and seminary, where students are expected to copy for future study, whole courses of lectures, there is a wide field for the use of a style rapid enuf for full notes, and easy enuf to be lerned and used by all. The lecturer must now either deliver his instruction with painful slownes, or the student must content himself with an abstract, rude and imperfect. Frequently the professor speaks one hundred and fifty, and more, words a minute; while the class follow him at the rate of twenty-five to thirty-five words a minute, getting, at the most, less than a quarter of the lecture, and that, too, of lectures prepared with the greatest care, and ex-prest in the most condenst language.

This difficulty has been frequently pointed out by professors of colleges, and other institutions of a high grade. Professor Nairne, of Columbia College, expreses, we think, a sentiment shared by most men in his position when he says, "For many years I hav desired to teach the students that lecturing is quite different from dictation of notes." They should be enabled "to report a lecture without interruption, even tho' it be delivered with the energy of a public discourse. Till they ar able to do this, instruction by lectures must be a very slow and tedius proces." And yet such is the proces of necesity followed in hundreds of institutions. Now, for this class of persons a style of brief writing is demanded that shall be sufficiently easy to be retained in the memory, and used to advantage, while the mind is intent upon the performance of other duties, to which the mere mechanical part of the writing is entirely subordinate. The Phonography of Mr. Pitman, and the styles derived from it, hav failed for these uses on account of too great complexity. Even after the practice of years has rendered familiar its irregular word-forms, they ar still felt to be a "burden," like the heavy armor of the ancients. To master its varied word and phrase forms was a work of years; and they were retained in memory by sheer force of inveterate habit, or by a peculiar tact that few persons possest. Added to these was another difficulty, equally great — viz., a want of perfect legibility. Whatever some experts may say to the contrary, Phonography has never been, and never can be, easy to read. Its reporting style omits nearly all the vowels, and supplies their place partially, and very obscurely, by means of devices which ar very burdensom, such as *positions* and peculiarity of outline. The rule of position (placing the word above, on, or below the line of writing) interrupted the continuity of the writing, broke up the phrases, and still failed to make many needed distinctions. There were, in some cases, a dozen words to be distinguisht, and only three positions, so that four words were represented by the same *form* in a given position, and twelv words by the same form in the diferent positions. The outline ⌒, for instance, was written (and is still written) for the following words: *eels, ills, isles, lees, lease, lies, allies; lace, lays, less, else, allays, lows, ails; laws, loose, lose, lass, alas, owls, allows,* and other words — making seven words to be represented by this one outline in each position, or more than twenty in all. Tho' it is not common for a single form to hav twenty and more words to represent, it is very common for a single outline to stand for *six, eight,* or even *twelv* words. The form ╲ is written for the words *post, pest, paced, past, opposed, weepest, hopest,* &c.; and the form ╲ for *taste, test, toast, attest, teased, tossed, eatest, aughtest,* &c. We need not multiply examples, but hundreds of them will occur to any one acquainted with Phonography.

In Tachygraphy, as here taught, all words of this class ar written distinctivly and with sufficient brevity by the use of a connected vowel where it is needed. In this way we avoid the use of the diferent *positions*, and gain, at the same time, a far higher degree of legibility than can be gained by resorting to this expedient.

But there ar dificulties that embaras the writer of Phonography, which ar far greater than those we hav mentioned above. The entire system of word-forms is based on the use of duplicate and triplicate signs, representing the same sounds or group of sounds. Frequently the same group of sounds may be exprest in *eight, ten,* or a *dozen* ways; while, on the other hand, five, six, or seven sounds may be combined into one complex sign, based on a single full-sized letter. Some of these devices ar useful in furnishing a variety of outline and brevity of form, and ar to be cultivated by the *profesional reporter*, so far as necessary for these purposes; but when this complexity reaches too high a degree, it becomes too burdensom, and places a style entirely beyond the reach of the class of persons whose wants we ar considering.

The complexity in Phonography growing out of its internal structure arises from — 1st, The use of several alphabetic forms for the same letter; and, 2d, Several modes of combining the same sounds into triple, quadruple, or quintuple stems.

1. The alphabetic forms most burdensom ar those for H, Y, and W. *H* has *four* modes of representation. *Y* combines with the vowels, assuming their positions and variations, making *twelv* signs which represent *y* with a following vowel (or, to speak more exactly, *four signs* varied by the three positions in such a way as to express twelv varieties of sound), and an additional sign employed in special cases. *W* has the *twelv variations*, with the vocals, as explained above, of *y*, and three more forms, — for *wi* (i long), *woi*, and *wou*, — and a *w*-hook on four of the consonants; making, with its own special sign, seventeen * variations, or, speaking of signs varied only by form and not by position, *eight* distinct signs to represent this one letter.

How Represented in Tachygraphy. — These sounds (the sounds of *W* and *Y*) ar exprest in Tachygraphy by only one sign, reducing their use to the most perfect simplicity, and cutting off the labor of many weeks in acquiring the style in the use of these letters alone.

2. *The Varius Modes of Combining the Same Sounds into* TRIPLE, QUADRUPLE, *or* QUINTUPLE STEMS.

We can give here only a brief illustration of the mode of contraction employed in Phonography, for a full explanation would require a treatise on the art. Our explanation cannot apply perfectly to the conflicting styles now known under the name Pho-

---

* It deservs mention, however, that some of the modern innovators upon Mr. Pitman's system hav endevord to limit the number of the forms for W and Y, and, in some cases, with partial success.

nography; but these styles hav, in this respect, about the same structure, and present nearly the same difficulties to the learner.

We take, by way of illustration, a single letter, applying to it a part of the *hooks*, *circles*, and *loops* by which it is modified in forming the system of contractions. *Ab uno disce omnes!* The same adjuncts apply to all the *straight* letters, while the curved letters lose some of these modes of contraction, and add others peculiar to themselves.

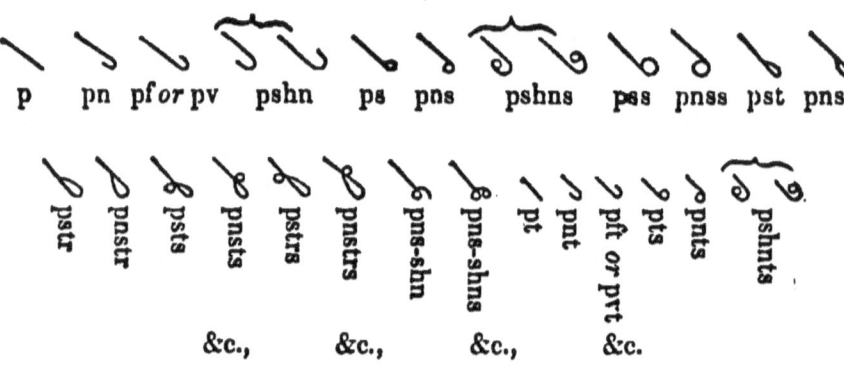

It would be too tedius to go thro' all the forms that this one letter assumes in combination; but the curius reader can fill up the list for himself by ading the final hooks, circles, and loops that ar attacht to the ⟍ in the illustrations above, to each of the following forms: —

This will make (after deducting those especially inconvenient) about 175* forms based on the letter *P*. Multiplying this num-

---

* Mr. Benn Pitman has given, in his "Reporter's First Reader," a table of compound stems, in which the compounds of the letter ⟍ amount to fifty-four, in place of the thirty-four given above, and the variations of the entire alphabet number about one thousand; but he

ber by eight (the number of straight signs to which such modifications belong), we get 1400 combinations. To these must be added the forms arising from the use of a part of these modes of contraction with the curved signs, and we get more than 2100 additional signs, or 3500 in all, composed of single stems with their modifications.

There is a degree of method in *forming* these complex stems that is worthy of praise, and should be duly appreciated; but there is no such method in their use, and it is not easy to employ the best form for a word when several possible forms occur to the mind. For example, suppose that a word containing the letters *s t r d* is to be written. The Phonographic letters are), |, / or ⌐, |. The form may be varied in more than a dozen ways, retaining the letters in the same order. In the following words, the only consonants written by the Phonographer ar *s t r d*; yet each word is written in a diferent way, as follows:—

Saturday, steward, stride, strayed, astrayed, astride, eastward, yesterday, sturdy, stirred, storied, star-eyed, asteroid

Were the forms given above all the forms from which the student must choose in writing words containing these letters, the difficulty

has given forms having hooks, or circles, or loops, on one end of the sign only, while a full table would contain forms in which the hooks, circles, &c., appear both singly on either end of the character, and doubly on both ends at the same time.

If it should be deemed sufficient to count the form of contraction only as it appears in its simpler form on each end of the stem separately, we should stil find more than a thousand stem-forms growing out of the alphabetic signs. The design in the text was, however, to give the number of forms in their full complement of initial and final hooks, circles, and loops, attacht as they actually appear in the written words.

would not be so great as it really is; for, besides these legitimate outlines, there are *eight* others,—

— which ar not recommended for use, yet ar quite as likely to be chosen by the young writer, who must choose between twenty possible outlines to find the correct one.

There ar other words, besides those given above, containing the same principal letters, for which word-forms must be provided from among those here given. So the only thing that can be done is to memorize the proper outline for the word, as we lern to spell in our common orthography, only with greater variations from general rules, and a greatly increast number of exceptional forms.

To acquire the Phonographic orthography is an almost endles labor. Mr. Graham has attempted to fathom this gulf, and to lay stepping-stones to aid the student, lest he sink in this Slough of Despond, and abandon the art in despair. He has provided a dictionary, indicating, by means of *type-keys*, as he calls them, the proper outline for *sixty thousand* words and *sixty thousand* phrases, making in all one hundred and twenty thousand* forms to be

---

* It should also be noticed that most of these forms of contraction ar not peculiar to the reporting style, but that the general principles of contraction apply also to the simplest style known to Phonography. The style used by reporters differs from the style offered for general use mainly in the addition of a few more irregularly contracted forms for words and phrases, and an omision of the vowels; while this immense fabric of *regular* contractions remains to be lerned by those who use the art even in its simplest form. And it is also worthy of remark that the same men who hav offered this complicated system to the public, hav, at the same time, complained long and loud of the anomalies of our English orthography, and hav taken the lead in the Phonetic reform. Yet our English orthography contains only about *two hundred and sixty digraphs and trigraphs*, which ar used as an extension to our alphabet; while the Phonographic orthography contains modified stems numbering, as we hav seen, more than *three thousand*. And we may, I presume, say with truth that

memorized. These forms can be of no use to the writer until rendered familiar by practice; and a hard-working student can master about one thousand forms a month, or the one hundred and twenty thousand in ten years, provided he takes no vacations, and can retain in memory such a mass of details. This system of word and phrase forms may be regarded as the first and second stories of the wonderful temple of modern Phonography. Above these rise other stories (or perhaps they should be likened to towers, since they ar formed of a far less amount of material), containing word and phrase signs contracted in a more irregular way, for which the general principles will not suffice. Mr. Graham, with his usual thoro'ness, has given about three thousand of these irregularly contracted forms.

In some of the styles of Phonography, forms still further removed from alphabetic principles ar found, device within device leading on to wonderful degrees of complexity, as where Mr. G., for instance, writes ⌊, which is literally *tft* or *tvd*, for *I hav;* or ⌇ for *of all*, and ⌒ for *of our;* while the former would naturally read *plt*, and the latter *prt*. Or, if the signs read *of all* and *of our* ar shorter than a halved letter, the diference between them and the halved letters cannot be more than one fiftieth of an inch — a distance wholly unappreciable by the eye, and impossible to be made in the hurry of reporting.

It is with no wish to criticise harshly the old Phonographies that we hav detailed these dificulties, that rise like mountains before the student. It is an unplesant task to deal in what seems, when stated in the mildest form, like severe censure. We hav refused for many years to expose the enormus asumptions of those who hav assumed ● lead the world in the stenographic arts, and actually hav controlled a large share of the public patronage in England and America, both as reporters and as teachers of short-hand. The

the diphthongal and triphthongal signs in our common spelling can be reduced to rule as easily as the compound stems in Phonography of which we hav spoken. Yet the Phonographers hav one advantage in point of consistency, if not of simplicity — they never employ silent letters, or combinations that hav no phonetic value whatever, as is the case in our long-hand orthography.

fact that some persons* hav succeeded in rising above all these difficulties, and in using systems so involved for the purposes of swift writing, is more creditable to the ability and perseverance of those persons who hav succeeded than to the systems they hav employed.

THE CONTRACTIONS USED IN TACHYGRAPHY.

But it remains for us to inquire how far, and in what way, this complexity of structure is avoided in Tachygraphy; or how sufficient brevity of word-forms is secured, for the use of persons desirus of securing full notes of lectures without resorting to so complex a system of outlines. To make the reply to these questions intelligible, it will be necessary to explain the *basis* upon which the system of contractions is built, and the principles followed in applying the different modes of shortening the word-forms. The student of the art will do well to take note of these principles, as they will enable him to understand why one form of contraction, in certain cases, is preferred to another, and why some ar rejected altogether.

Contractions may be of several degrees of complexity. For the sake of distinction, we will call those forms that express sounds accurately and naturally Pure Phonic Contractions; those of the second grade, Mixed Phonic; and those of the third grade, Stenographic.†

---

* The number of persons who hav succeeded in mastering Phonography, so as to be really expert, is much fewer than is generally supposed, as was stated in the Introduction to the Elements of Tachygraphy, page 22. We estimated at that time (1869) the number of competent reporters at five hundred persons in England and America, and conceded a greater or less degree of skill in the art to two thousand persons more. These figures hav not yet been called in question, altho' they hav been before the public nearly three years. We think the estimate rather too large than too small, and that the number is not increasing. There has been certainly a prodigious waste of time and effort on the part of thousands of persons; and yet this result is quite as favorable as would be naturally expected in the use of such a system as we hav shown Phonography to be.

† This classification is not designed to be exhaustiv, but will answer the purpose of illustration for which it is intended.

PHONIC SIGNS—L AND R SERIES.   19

Pure Phonic Signs.

Abbreviations of the first grade are those given in the seventh chapter of the "Elements," page 71, where signs ar provided for the consonantal diphthongs of the *L* and *R* series, as follows :—

bl pl gl cl fl   br pr gr cr   dr tr   fr thr shr

Here the *L* and the *R* blend with the preceding consonant, and unite, forming a compound sound, as in the words *play* and *pray*. Now, this form of contraction is definitely limited, both in the number of its forms and the frequency of their use, by the structure of the language written. There ar in English only the fourteen compounds named above, of which *L* and *R* form part in this intimate union. But there ar sounds in final syllables, as in the last syllables of the words *people* and *peeper*, that may be classed with these without too much violation of the principles of phonics. All the signs given above ar sometimes used in this manner, and in addition to them the following, which ar never purely phonic signs :—

dl tl vl nl vr zhr thr   nr zhl shl

These, with the fourteen signs before named, make twenty-four signs of the *L* and *R* series. These ar all the signs * that can be made of this kind without decending to the third grade of contractions. The letters *yl, hl, wl, ll*, and some others, which Mr. Munson unites into one sign, hav no phonic union even of the remotest kind. Herein the introduction of such signs does not tend to ren-

---

* It might be possible to add to the signs given above others to represent *sl* and *zl*, but these ar provided more naturally in connection with the *S* series mentioned below. *Jr* and *chr* ar also provided with signs of this series, but they ar the same as *zhr* and *shr* ; and *jl* and *chl* ar of but little use.

der the system uniform, as he seems to suppose, but introduces an anomalism into it; for, having provided *signs* for which he has no corresponding *sounds* in the language, he must employ them in an arbitrary manner. It is scarcely possible in this way to determine when *yl*, for instance, shall be written with the full form or with the hooked form, as there ar *no cases* in which the latter ar needed. In endevoring, therefore, to produce uniformity by adding initial hooks to all the letters of the alphabet to represent *l* and *r*, Mr. Munson has succeeded only in producing an external uniformity to which there is no corresponding internal reality, and consequently has produced confusion in the use of all the signs of this class.

Phonic Signs of the S Series.

The signs of this series, unlike those given above, may represent either the union of *s* with a following or a preceding consonant. The only purely phonic signs of this class ar —

sp sk st sf sn sl sw

ps ks ts fs ths ns ls rs

Connected with the latter of these series is the use of the circle to represent *z* after hevy signs, as follows : —

bz gz dz vz thz mz nz lz rz

These, in their proper use, ar purely phonic signs, an l ar used in the First Style of Tachygraphy. They number twenty-five, and, with the twenty-four given above as belonging to the *L* and *R* series, give us forty-nine (to which may be added the ⸗ , making fifty) diphthongal signs. These ar all the compound letters that ar used in the First Style of Tachygraphy as taught in the "Elements;" and their use is, for the most part, definite and natural. There is a striking contrast between these fifty signs of the first grade and the thirty-five hundred used in Phonography, the larger part of which ar of the second or third grade. And yet the fifty signs given in the First Style of Tachygraphy, together with the few word and phrase signs used, furnish a style more rapid than the Corresponding Style of the old art, with all its complexity. Only a small rate of speed can be gained in Phonography without omitting the vowels; and when the student has omitted the vowels, he must master the whole system of *outlines* in order to read his writing with any certainty, which, as we hav shown, is the labor of years.

First Result.

We hav, then, as the first result, a style in Tachygraphy for which Phonography affords no parallel, and for which it can form no parallel without an entire change of structure — a style that can be used as freely and legibly as our common script, and reduced to practice as redily; while it is written three times as rapidly, and with less than one seventh of the labor. Such a result is in itself enuf to commend the system. But, in achieving this, we hav, at the same time, secured the best basis upon which to build the briefer styles demanded by the *note-taker* and *reporter*.

The Contractions of the Note-taker's Style.

In forming a briefer style than that sketcht above, there ar several modes of abbreviating the writing. The first and most obvius mode is that of providing brief signs to represent words and phrases of frequent occurrence. There ar some words that occur many times on every page of writing, and a list of one hundred words may be made that will form a large *per centum* of the words employed in ordinary writing. Such words ar — *A, an, and, are, as, at, be, by, come, did, do, done, for, from, go, had, has, hav, he, his, how, I, if, in, is, it, on, one, so, some, that, the, then, there, they, this, though, us, was, we, were, what, when, where, who, you, your,* &c. By furnishing these words with the briefest available signs, the labor of writing is reduced in a very simple and easy way. This principle of abbreviation has been understood from the erliest times, and may be redily applied to any language.

Another principle immediately connected with this, tho' not used so anciently, is that of providing brief signs for the most frequently recurring phrases, such as *have been, has been, there is, it is, this is, it was, to be, to hav, to do,* &c. Great advantage is gained by uniting such phrases into one character, which may be done by simply joining the word-signs used for the simple words.

These principles form part of all systems that hav any value at the present day.

Most of the words of this class ar provided with brief signs in the First Style of Tachygraphy; and some others become brief enuf thro' those principles of contraction which ar of general application. A few, however, ar specially contracted, and from some of them numerus derivativs ar formed, which ar written in analogy with their primitivs, thus reducing even the word-signs to some degree of regularity. The most frequent phrases ar also provided with brief signs, either by simply uniting the word-signs, or by further abbreviating them. A skilful use of these word and phrase signs, in addition to the brief forms of the First Style, would give considerable speed to the writing, and might be sufficient for some persons. Yet there ar many long words in that portion of our language which is derived from the Latin and the Greek that may be further abbreviated to advantage. These words ar built up from a *root* or *stem* word by the addition of prefixes and affixes; as, for example, *inter-communication,* which may be divided into *inter-com-munica-tion.* By providing brief signs to represent the prefixes *inter-* and *com-*, and the termination *-tion,* we greatly reduce the labor of writing; thus, ⌇⌇⌇ , *intercommunication.*

Prefix Signs.

The general principles of contraction afford brief signs for most of the prefixes, yet there ar a few that ar provided with special signs. Some of these, such as *com-, con-,* and *in-,* form part of thousands of words, which renders it possible to effect a shortening in all these words by the use of only a few brief forms representing prefixes. So also with the *affixes.*

Affix Signs.

The *terminations* of words which require any special devices for contraction ar very few, and apply to thousands of words; so that the use of a dozen brief signs for *affixes*, in connection with the *prefix* signs mentioned above, abbreviates the writing to an extent that is a continual wonder, even tho' so long known and used. (See Chapters VII. and VIII.)

We hav thus provided for the representation, in a brief manner, of — 1st, The words of most frequent occurrence; and, 2d, For words of Latin and Greek origin, composed largely of derivativs from some common stem-word. But there is another class of words in our language, and one of great use and importance, that is not reacht in this way.

Common Saxon Words.

We refer to the great body of Saxon words which form the staple of ordinary intercourse. They present few markt features of regularity, and cannot be shortened in so simple a manner as those composed of prefixes and affixes. They abound in consonant letters, employing not unfrequently four or five such letters in a single syllable; as, for instance, *strand, starts, plants*.

We hav shortened these words materially by the use of the signs of the *L, R,* and *S* series, heretofore explained; and it may be doubted whether we can carry the process of contraction farther without more loss than gain. Yet, theoretically, wherever two consonants are frequently joined without an intervening vowel, a sign may be used to represent them in combination. Such combinations ar *-rd, -nd, -ld,* &c., in *hard, hand, hold; -rt, -lt,* and *-nt,* in *hurt, hilt,* and *hunt*. And in like manner *r* and *l* may unite with almost any consonant following them, as in *harsh, surf, elf, elm*. But some of these combinations ar much more important than others; for, while *f, m,* and *sh* may unite with a preceding *l* or *r* only, the *d* and *t* may unite with nearly all the consonant letters of the same degree of hardness, as *z* and *s* do in the list of final compounds of the *S* series. Hence, by adopting one mode of contracting all letters which combine with *d* or *t*, we gain a multitude of brief forms growing out of one principle. To represent this union of *d* and *t* with a preceding consonant, the consonant which precedes is shortend,* and the *d* or *t* is thus indicated without being written.

The other combinations named hav never been furnished with any briefer signs than the alphabet provides. There is, however, another step that may be taken in the formation of shortened forms. Having signs for the consonantal diphthongs of the *L*, *R*, and *S* series (both initial and final), and of the *d* and *t* series final, these brief signs may be used to represent the same letters when not united diphthongally. For instance, the ꜰ may be used in the words *soap, soup, sup, sap, sop*, as well as *spy;* the ꜰ in the words *bill, bell, ball, able*, as well as *blow, blew*, and *blue*, and so on through all the signs that represent consonants in union. This practice opens the way for entire licentiusnes of word-forms. It substitutes for the alphabetic signs others to be used in their place — not merely in certain well-defined cases of combinations, but in any case where the fancy of the writer may choose to use them. Such licentiusnes could not be tolerated, as it would throw the whole system into confusion.† And the only escape from it, after once

---

* This method of representing *d* and *t* when united with a preceding consonant (and the same form of contraction has been largely used also in other cases) is an important feature of all the Phonographies, and its utility as a stenographic device cannot be doubted. Yet it has been severely criticised as wanting in definitnes, and requiring too much precision in the writer. These objections are valid if applied to a style for general use, but form no very insuperable objection against a style for reporters, which must avail itself of brief forms in some manner. Before the half-length characters are abandond, better ones must be provided. We regard them as entirely satisfactory, if limited in their use to the cases of phonic union specified, or when extended in a simple and natural way to the addition of a *t* after a light character, and a *d* after a hevy character; but when a light or hevy character is allowed to indicate either a *d* or *t* at plesure, and a hook is added to the shortend letter to represent *nd* or *nt*, *shnd* or *shnt*, *vd* or *ft*, the complexnes is greatly increast, and the original design seems to be buried in its accessories. However necessary this may be in the most involved of reporting styles, it certainly has no proper place either in a style for general writing, or in a simple style for note-taking.

† The confusion actually resulting from this licentius use of the con-

adopting the principle, is by assigning, more or less arbitrarily, one mode of contraction to one word, and another mode to another, and teaching the proper outlines individually. This method was resorted to in Phonography; but we hav preferd, in this style, to use those methods of contraction principally in their first and legitimate sphere. We hav, however, treated the *circle* as a substitute for the alphabetic *S*, employing it with great freedom in long words, but restricting its use in words of one syllable sufficiently to render the outlines distinctiv.

The use of the half-length characters of the *d* and *t* series is also extended somewhat beyond the cases mentioned on page 23, but they ar employed with greater restriction than in the old style.

The lengthened curves ar introduced; but their use is confined mainly to the prefixes *enter-* and *inter-*, and to a few words of frequent occurrence. We hav thus reduced the number of contracted stem-forms to about *five hundred*, or one seventh of the *thirty-five hundred* used in Phonography, and, by employing them in a more natural manner, hav renderd those introduced far easier of application.

Rapidity of Writing Secured.

Having secured so good a degree of simplicity, some persons will desire to know something concerning the rate of speed secured. While the rate of speed has been held subordinate to the more essential qualities of *legibility* and *simplicity*, it has not been overlookt. Indeed, in securing simple and facile forms, we hav, at the same time, secured forms most easily and rapidly written. There will always be great diversity of talent shown in the ability to write rapidly by persons using the same style, but there is quite as much diversity in the

Rate of Public Speaking.

The average rate of public speaking has long been regarded as about one hundred and twenty words a minute. But many good

tractions was, and still is, very great among Phonographers. A given page is often written with very different word-forms by students using the same text-book.

speakers speak slower than this, and quite as many faster than this. The slowest speakers utter seventy-five to one hundred words a minute, and the most rapid from one hundred and sixty to two hundred words, or even faster than this for one or two minutes at a time. Yet rapid speakers do not always speak so rapidly, and the slowest sometimes accelerate their speed to an average rate. The rate of both speakers and writers is generally estimated for a period of only a few minutes at a time. Estimated by the hour, the speed diminishes considerably. This style is written at the rate of one hundred and twenty to one hundred and fifty words a minute, and may be carried beyond this rate of speed by skilful men. Indeed, it is difficult to set a definit limit to the power of such a style. Used with the freedom with which we write the ordinary script, its speed would be at least six times as great. Our common script is written at the rate of twenty to forty words a minute. It will thus be seen that we gain for practical purposes more speed than is gained in Phonography by any except the few professional writers.

Second Result.

We hav thus, as a second result of the simplification of the system, produced a style adequate for taking full reports of ordinary speeches, sermons, or lectures, while at the same time it is very accurate and legible. We hav gaind this result in a style so simple, that students in all our professional schools and colleges can reduce it to practice without interrupting their other studies, and in a reasonably short space of time.*

The Reporting Style.

We cannot treat here of the contractions peculiar to the Reporting Style of Tachygraphy. Those that devote their lives to the art can afford to spend a longer time in preparing for their work, and, thro' long practice, may become skilled in a greater number

---

* Students ar able to put the First Style to practical use with two or three months' study, and can master the Second Style in two months additional, without interrupting their other pursuits. By devoting their whole time, they may lern them sooner than this.

of peculiar and irregular word-forms; but, even among professional reporters, there is a limit to the degree of complexity that can be made practical. M. Gouraud * has well said: —

"Whoever has attempted to lern any of the systems encumberd with these exceptional intricacies" [referring to those used in Phonography] "must hav experienced this unavoidable consequence — viz., that, whenever an excess of exertion in the memory has been brought in to aid the fingers, the progres of the student has always been retarded.† Indeed, experience has often proved that the most lengthy kind of writing" [the writer doubtles means a comparativly extended style of brief writing] "could *sooner* help, in its fullest delineation, to follow the delivery of a voluble orator, than the most condenst or abbreviated system of reporting stenography."

We shall treat further concerning the wants of professional reporters in our next volume, devoted to the Reporting Style. But, whatever reporters as a class may need in a system of brief writing, there can be no question that students, lawyers, editors, and literary men of most classes, demand *simplicity* and *legibility*, and only so much brevity as is consistent with these more essential qualities of good writing.

* See work entitled " Cosmo-phonography," by Francis F. Gouraud, D. E. S., New York, 1850, page 179.

† It is on this account that the speed of writing does not increase in proportion to the brevity of the style. In actual practice, the speed of the writing may diminish as briefer forms ar introduced; and when the briefer forms ar so mastered as to add somewhat to the speed of the writing, it is always far less than would be anticipated, for there is always a loss growing out of the increased complexity to be deducted from the gain growing out of the brevity. Hence it is that we increase the number of the brief forms of the First Style four-fold in order to double the speed of the writing, and must increase them in as great a ratio to add fifty per cent. of speed to the style here given. As, in ascending high mountains, the steepnes of the way increases with each degree of progres, so, in brief writing, it is vastly easier to gain a speed of one hundred and twenty to one hundred and forty words a minute than to increase this speed to one hundred and eighty or two hundred words. Yet even this highest rate of speed is attainable in Tachygraphy, and has been attained by some persons.

Acknowledgments. — It would be unjust to close this Introduction without repeating the acknowledgments previusly made to those who hav done so much, in former years, to develop and perfect the art of brief writing. Their labors, however imperfect, were necessary; and, though we must add to their work a little here, and take from it a little there, yet it has formd a basis without which none of the present systems could hav been produced.

The author would acknowledge especial obligations to the distinguisht Inventor of Phonography, Isaac Pitman, Esq., of England, in whose works he first lernd to love the art of swift writing, and whose patient and long-continued devotion to the development of the principles of the science has done so much to enrich it with new and valuable material. The new letters were not adopted through any love of novelty, but only because the art could not be rendered practicable without them; and it is a source of plesure to the author of Tachygraphy that he is conscius of laboring in entire sympathy with all the aspirations and hopes awakend by the introduction of Phonography into this country, more than a quarter of a century ago. He believes that these hopes will be realized in the introduction of Tachygraphy. Though changed in form and dress, the essential principles remain; and the art, in its new form, embodies in a practical manner what was foreshadowd in the old. Thus men labor as grace and wisdom ar given them from above, but God directs for his own glory and the good of men. He is the true INVENTOR.

THE NOTE-TAKER.

CHAPTER I.

SHORTENED WORD-FORMS.

1. The abbreviations employed in this style of Tachygraphy may be classed under the following divisions: 1st, Word-signs; 2d, General Contractions; 3d, Prefixes and Affixes; 4th, Phrase-signs.

WORD-SIGNS.

2. *Definition.* — A word-sign is a Tachygraphic word-form shortened by omitting or contracting some of the letters used in writing it fully. Word-signs are formed by special and sometimes irregular modes of contraction, which apply only to the words specified, or to their derivatives.

The characters used for word-signs are,—
a, Letters of the Tachygraphic alphabet.
b, Compound signs. *c*, Combined signs.
d, Contracted and Irregular signs.

3. Word-signs may be further classed as — A, Vocal, B, Consonantal signs. The purely Vocal signs are found only in Class *a*.

Class *b* consists of the secondary letters of the L, R, and S series of compounds.

Class *c* may contain either a consonant and a vowel, or two or more consonants.

Class *d* comprises word-signs formed, in part, of letters which do not appear in the word as written in the full form, or those which employ one or more of the final letters of the word.

REMARK.— The latter class is very small, and forms an exception to the general principles which are followed almost uniformly throughout the system.

4. Word-signs may be further classed into Primitives and Derivatives.

A Primitive word-sign is the simplest form in which it occurs. as **1**, object; **⌐**, will. A Derivative word-sign is any modification of such Primitive form.

5. We add a table of the Primitive word-signs that are of the most frequent occurrence.

CHAPTER I.   31

TABLE OF WORD-SIGNS.

A. — 1. Vocal Signs.

⌒ ye   - who   ⌃ all   ⟋ how
⊃ in   ᴜ have   ⟍ of   - or ǀ the

B. — Consonantal Signs.

2. *Common Abbreviations.*

c∣ A.B.   ⌐ Co.   ⁄ Mr.
c — A.D.   -- D.D.   ⌒ Math.
c⌒ A.M.   ⌐ Dep.   ∣⌒ P.S.
⟍ Acc.   ⌐ Do.   ∣⌒ P.M.
⌐⌐ Chap.   ⌣ Eng.   ⌒ Rev.

3. *In which only Vocals are omitted.*

∣ Be   ⌊ they   ⟋ are
∣ up   ⌐ though   ⌒ we
⟍ go   ⌠ may   ⌣ you
⌒ us, so   ⌣ on, own   ⌒ he

4. *In which both Vocals and Consonantals are omitted.*

1	object		thing
	subject		number
	principle, -al		neverthelesss
	improve		knowledge
	perhaps		language
	together		represent
	Tachygraphy		remark
	value		with
	form		general
	Phonography		gentlemen (an)

5. *Irregular Forms.*

	advantage		notwithstanding
	&c.		pleasure
	as		question
	because		when
	each		while
	hath		which
	him		whole
	large		will

CHAPTER I.

EXPLANATION OF THE TABLE.

6. *a.* The first list of word-signs, composed wholly of vocal signs, are used in forming compounds and phrases, in the same way as the vocals are used in forming outlines for words.

Examples.

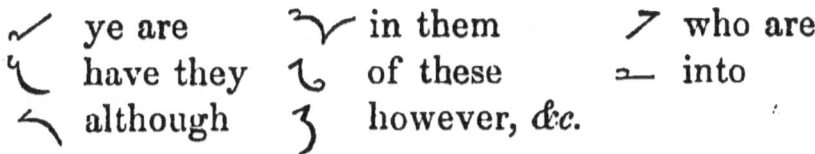

    ye are   in them   who are
    have they   of these   into
    although   however, *&c.*

b. It should be particularly noticed, however, that the sign for the article *the* may be written either perpendicularly or horizontally, and that it *never stands alone.* All other vocal word-signs may be written either joined or disjoined; the tick for *the* is always joined. It may commence or end a phrase.

Examples.

    the way   the time
    the advantage   the favor
    in the   to the
    as the   by the, *&c.*

7. *a.* The second list of signs are always written independently, as they stand in the table. They are not purely phonic signs, but are so suggestiv of the common abbreviations, universally used, as to need no special memorizing. Their use may be learned by an examination of the table. It will be noticed, however, that such abbreviations as have no phonetic value — as, for instance, *Kt.* for *Knight* — are omitted from the table. It would not do to write ⌣ for *Knight.*

REMARK. — It will be observed that the sign for A. in A. B. and A. D. expresses different sounds in *Artis Bachelor* and *Anno Domini*, and that A. M. may be written for *Artis Magister* and *Ante Meridiem*, as well as for *Anno Mundi.*

b. LIST NO. 3. — Words of a single consonant letter need, for the most part, a vowel to make them perfectly legible. It would not do to confound such words as *any, no, now, nay, know, own*, &c., nor is it at all necessary. *Any* and *now* are written ⌣ and ⌣; and other words which contain only the consonant ⌣, except *on* and *own*, add the vowel. In a similar way, all little words of this class are treated. The following words, for instance, may be written in this Style as they are written in the First Style: *Bow, bough, ape, ope, gay, see, say, thee, aim, mow, me, my, ray, row, raw, ear, oar, way, woe, nay, high,* &c.

c. Number 4 contains contractions from which many derivative forms spring. It is arranged, as the preceding table is, in the order of the Tachygraphic alphabet. The signs derived from these will be given in another chapter.

8. The last number contains anomalous forms, from the most of which no other forms are derived.

a. In the sign for *each,* the hook of the ⌒ is omitted.

b. The sign for *as* is the *s*-circle. The common abbreviation *&c.* is written with the halved ⌣ used for *and,* and ⌒, and reads *and-so-forth.*

c. The stems of the letters *Hu* and *Wha* are omitted in the words *hath, whole, while, when,* and *him,* and the hook only is written.

d. In the word-signs *advantage* and *large,* (is used for ⌒, as being more distinctive and convenient to write.

REMARK.—In memorizing the tables, let the student write each word-sign over many times, and repeat the word as the character is made. When the signs are learned so that they can be written correctly, they may be written from the lips of a reader, repeating each sign and each table of signs many times, until they can be written with great rapidity and skill.

WRITING EXERCISE FIRST.

Short Sentences containing Word-signs.

Com unto me, all ye that labor! How shal they giv who hav not? In this rejoice! The way of the rihteus is as a shining liht. The day, the time, the path, the goal, the glory, the ground, the place, the praise. In the, on the, for the, to the, tho' the, thro' the, hav the, all the. John Jones, A. B. A. D. 1872. Adam Smith, A. M., in acc. with Samuel Sampson, D. D. Mr. William Howland, Deputy P. M. General, Washington, D. C. E. Dow, B. A., Prof. of Mathematics, Cambridge, Eng. Perhaps the principal object in our meeting together is to consider the subject in all its bearings. Gentlemen may remark the value of Tachygraphy as contrasted with Phonography in the expression of language, and they will form an opinion in accordance with the facts. A knoledge of the principles of language is of general utility. Notwithstanding the advantages of the mesure, a large number of gentlemen wer disposed to call it in question. To him that hath shal be given, and from him that hath not shal be taken even that which he seemeth to hav. Becaus I hav calld and ye hav refused, I hav stretcht out my hands all the day long, and no man regarded, &c. It is as each one shal choose. Tho' the whole juruy gav us plesure in the main, we wer nevertheles delihted when we reacht our homes. They hav taken advantage of your remarks. A large number of persons wer present. Wud you be wise, five things observ with care — of whom you speak, to whom you speak, and how, and when, and where.

CHAPTER II.

THE USE OF THE CIRCLE.

9. The *circle* is retained in the Note-Taker's style in all cases in which it is used in the first style of Tachygraphy.

The *circle* is used in the first style,—

a. In all initial and final compounds containing *s*, and with the *dot vocal*, as in

b. With other short and obscure vowels, especially in words of more than one or two syllables. (See Elements, pp. 71, 78, and 79.)

10. In the Note-Taker's style, the use of the circle is farther extended, as specified below.

1. The circle is used with all single vowels in most words of more than two consonants, and with a larger number of short words than in the first style.

2. Words of *two* consonant letters, one of which is *s*, and some words of *three* consonants, require much limitation in the use of the circle. Since the same consonant skeleton may be vocalized to form a dozen, and in some

cases many more different, words, the use of vocal signs is necessary to secure definiteness in the writing; and the vocal frequently precludes the use of the circle. (See 12, 3, Rem. 1.)

3. Many words of three consonants, however, and nearly all words of four and more, are sufficiently definite from their consonant outline alone, and admit of contraction with more freedom.

11. *a.* Words of two consonant letters, one of which is *s*, are quite numerous. The different words growing out of a single pair of consonant letters form, in some cases, a group of twenty, thirty, or more words which must be distinguished either by difference of outline or by vocalization. Hence it is necessary to limit the use of the *circle* in such classes of words, even in the briefest style of the art.

b. The use or disuse of the circle in such cases depends upon the number of words in the *group*, and the frequency with which any given word is employed. Hence general rules cannot be applied satisfactorily.

12. The following specifications will aid the student to understand the use of the circle in words of only two or three consonant letters.

1. With the consonant letters *l-s* and the vowels are formed more than thirty words, as follows: *ails, alas,*

CHAPTER II. 39

alias, allays, alleys, allies, allows, alloys, awls, eels, Elias, Ellis, else, eyeless, isles, lace, lass, lays, laws, lease, lees, less, Lewis, lice, lows, loose, lose, loss, louse, oils, owls, &c.

NOTE.—For key to the proper forms of these words, see Reading-Lesson Third, 4.

REM.—Phonographers write ⌒ as the outline for all of these words, which leads to great indefiniteness in reading. Or, if the disjoined vowel is added, there is a greater loss of speed than in writing the word in the fullest form, as in the first style of the art.

2. This group of words may be taken as a type of many similar groups which contain only two consonants, one of which is *s;* such as *r-s, m-s, p-s, s-n, s-l, s-p,* &c. Thus the circle is used in the words *airs, errs, oars, ours, ears,* and *erse;* and the full form in the words *race, rice, rouse, rise, arise, areas, iris, houries,* &c. (Read. Les. Third, 5.)

So, also, we use the circle in *muss* and *mess, aims* and *alms,* but vocalize *amaze. amuse, mice, mouse, moose;* the circle in *pass, apes, opes,* and the longer form in *pace, pause, pose, pews, poise, paws, pease, oppose.* (R. L. Third, 6.)

3. Many other groups of words are written in analogy with these.

REM. 1.—The vowel is often omitted when the ⌒ or ⌒ is written, and in this respect these outlines differ from the forms used for these words in the first style. The vocal ⊂ before ⌒ is almost always omitted, conforming to the general rule that vocal signs are omitted when they are not easily joined; and the ∩ before ⌒ and ⌒ is almost always written in words of this class.

REM. 2.—Words belonging to such groups as those mentioned above, if of frequent occurrence, should be written as briefly as is consistent with perfect legibility. If the word contains an initial vowel which can be written, the circle may be used with the greater freedom, as in the words *allays, allows.* Still, even here there must be some restriction, for we have also the words *alloys, allies,* and *alleys* to be distinguished from them.

REM. 3.— The words containing *l-s,* and similar groups which end in a vowel, *lazy, Lucy, boozy, fussy,* &c. have not been given in the preceding lists because they all conform to the general principle which prescribes the use of ⌒ and ⌢ in all cases where *s* is the last consonant in the word, and followed by a vowel.

13. In all words, long as well as short, the ⌒ or ⌢ is used for *s,*—

a. Where this letter is immediately preceded or followed by a diphthong, or by two vocals, as in the words *disguise, espouse, disabuse, science, serious.* (R. L. Third, 7.)

b. Where a vocal precedes *s* or *z* in the beginning of a word, or follows them in the end of a word, as in the words *essential, fancy.*

EXCEPTION 1.— Where ᴗ or ╱ commences a word followed by *s*, the circle is sometimes joined to, or written within, the vocal, as in

ask, auspicious.

Exc. 2.— A final vowel may also be written after the circle in such words as

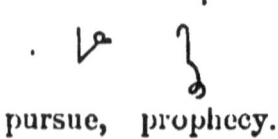

pursue, prophecy.

In this case, however, when another consonant is added, the vowel is dropped, as in

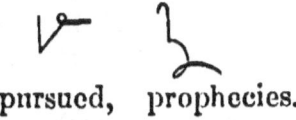

pursued,   prophecies.

SPECIFICATION.—The following words of frequent occurrence are written with the circle: *case, seen, south, this, use* (noun), *house*.

REM. 1.—The circle is not used in *scene* or *seine*. It must not be supposed that when a word is contracted irregularly that all words pronounced in a similar manner follow the same analogy. One word may be contracted on account of frequent occurrence, while another word, both spelled and pronounced in the same manner, is written in full. The word *will*, as a noun, as in the phrase *the will of God*, is written as in the common style of the art, while the word-sign ⟩ is used only for the auxiliary *will* in such phrases as *He will go*. This principle will be observed in other instances.

REM. 2.—The use of the circle in long words is considerably extended. It is restricted only by the following principles:—

a. Where a vowel follows s *in the end of a word, or precedes it in the commencement.* To this principle there are no exceptions, except those noticed above in connection with the vowels ⌣ and / in the beginning of a word, and two or three vowels in the end of a word.

b. Where the s *in the midst of the word is either preceded or followed by two vocals or a diphthong*, as, for instance, in the last syllables of the words *spontaneous, erroneous, harmonious, counterpoise*. (R. L. Fourth, 9.)

To this principle there are some exceptions, which are mentioned below.

REM. 3.—The circle is used in long words wherever it is more convenient than the full form, even with the double vocals and diphthongs, if the resulting outline is entirely legible, and not liable to be confounded with any other word.

Examples.—*Licentiate, licentious.* So, also, in the words *unsound, assign*, &c.

Rem. 4. — The circle is used in certain terminations ending in *s* preceded by two vowels, as, for instance, *uous* in the words *ambiguous, impetuous, tempestuous*, &c. (R. L. Fourth, 9.)

Rem. 5. — No account is made of silent vowels. When several vowels occur, only one of which is sounded, the vowel is considered as single.

The word *gorgeous*, for instance, though ending in a syllable which contains three vowels, is pronounced as though there were but one, and is written with the circle.

Rem. 6. — The above principles and directions will, it is hoped, make the use of the circle plain in most cases. If some cases still occur, in which the proper word-form is doubtful, the student must rely upon his observation in reading Tachygraphy, or the judgment of a competent teacher. The correction of exercises written by the pupil, in which words embodying these principles occur, is the best way of mastering them in detail.

THE CIRCLE FOR Z.

14. In addition to the principles given in the Elements for the use of the circle for *z*, it may be used, —

a. In long words generally, when not precluded by the principles before mentioned; but it cannot be used when the word begins with *z*.

Spec. 1. *a.* — The circle is used in such words as *deserve, observe, desert, resort*, &c., where the sound of *z* seems to be a necessity of speech.

b. The long sign ⌒ is used, however, in *zeal, zany,* &c. where the *z* is initial; also in *business, emblazon, season,* and wherever the circle might be read for *s*.

2. — Some cases of doubtful outlines will occur; and

CHAPTER II. 43

some words may be distinguished in writing that have the same consonants similarly situated. The words *reason, risen, rosin, raisin,* for instance, contain the same consonant elements, but they may be distinguished as follows.

a. In the following pairs of words, *reside recede, preside precede,* and others of this character, there is a double reason for writing the former word of the pair in the full form. These words contain both the z and the diphthong v in connection with it; and so there is a stronger reason for writing *reside* and *preside* in full than for writing *recede* and *precede* in full. So, *recede* and *precede* are written with the circle, and *reside* and *preside* with ⌒.

b. Some persons may also wish to distinguish more accurately between such words as *precede* and *proceed,* and to separate these in outline from *praised* and *prized.* The latter group (*praised* and *prized*) are written with the halved ⌒, explained in chapter IV, and the former (*proceed* and *precede*) may be distinguished by adding the vowel if necessary to one of the words.

c. In most *long words* no confusion can result from freedom in the use of the circle for *z;* and, yet, in a few cases, like *president* and *precedent,* perfect perspicuity requires a restricted use of the circle. Such instances can be fully specified only in a vocabulary; but persons who do not require the briefest forms, and who need great accuracy in writing, can easily avoid all difficulty by using the long ⌒ in all cases where the circle might be taken for *s.*

d. The terminations *ism* and *asm* in words of two syllables may frequently be written with the circle when preceded by a consonant, and in some cases when preceded by a vowel, as in

theism, baptism, methodism, agrarianism.

b. The circle is used for *z* in the following words: *does, these, was, use* (verb), *his, has.*

SPEC.—The word *was* takes the ⌒ in some phrases for convenience, and the full form is quite as rapid as the shorter form when both are equally convenient. The form with the circle is needed in such phrases as *was not, was done,* and is quite convenient in *was so* and *was this.* The full form is more convenient in the phrases *I was sure, was present,* and others of this kind. (R. L. Fourth, 8.)

c. The circle is used for *z* in forming the plural of nouns and third persons singular of verbs, which are represented by word-signs. Thus the circle is added to the word-signs for *improve, represent, form, advantage, principle,* &c., making *improves, represents, forms, advantages, principles,* &c.

SPEC.—Where the first form of the verb ends in a consonant, the circle will be added to all classes of words in forming the plural of the noun and third person singular of the verb; but where the first form of the word ends in a vowel, there will be some restriction of this principle. Yet words of frequent occurrence will attract the briefer form, as, for instance, *goes, days.*

REM. 1.— This principle should not be carried too far. There would be no advantage arising from writing such words as *ways* or *weighs* with the circle; it would lead to indefiniteness with no proportionate gain in speed.

REM. 2. — In the reporting style, a larger class of words is contracted in this way, and provision is made for the increased frequency of the use of certain words in special kinds of reporting. Such details must be reserved for the treatise on that style.

THE DOUBLE CIRCLE.

15. The circle is made twice its usual size to represent *s-s* with any intervening vowel, and may be thickened to represent *s-z*.

a. The double circle is chiefly used to express the syllables *ses*, *sis*, *sus*, *sez*, and *siz* in words like the following:—

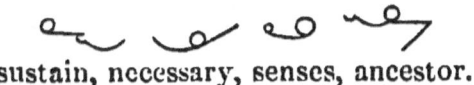
sustain, necessary, senses, ancestor.

b. It may also be used in a few cases where a long vowel or a diphthong occurs between the *s*'s; but with these vowels the fully-written forms are generally better, as

Cæsar, Alsace.

SPEC. 1.— The double circle may be used with great freedom; but it is sometimes more convenient to write the long sign for one of the *s*'s, even where there is no rule to prevent the use of the double circle, as in

Cicero, Cæsarea, recess, races.

2. — The use of the double circle cannot be fully understood until the student has learned the use of the half-length and double-length principles taught in chapters IV and V. The words *system* and *sister*, for instance, would be naturally written with the double circle, but it is thought better to write the former of these words with a shortened ⌒, and the latter with a lengthened ⌢. (See Chap. IV., sec. 40, *a*, and Chap. V, sec. 48, *c*, Spec.)

3. — The rules already given for the use of the *circle* will aid the student in the use of the *double circle*, for the presence of a diphthong, or two vowels immediately before or after the *s*'s, precludes its use, since one of the *s*'s must be written with the long sign, as in

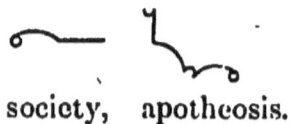

society, apotheosis.

4. — In some cases the double circle is used in a derivative word when it does not occur in the primitive form, as, for instance,

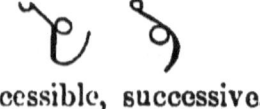

accessible, successive,

while the words *access* and *success* do not have it.

5. — The double circle may be used in the word o⎯ (*assist*), ignoring the vowel which begins the word, though this form of contraction is not allowed in many cases of this kind.

S BEFORE COMPOUNDS OF THE R-SERIES.

16. *a.* When *s* precedes the compounds  the circle is written on the *r-hook* side, and the *r* is thereby implied, as in the words

stream, screen, spring, supper, sadder.

b. When these forms occur in the midst of a word, as in *express, describe, restrain,* the hook will appear.

restrain, subscribe, express, describe, prosper, distress.

c. There are some cases, however, in which the *triple* compounds *spr, str, scr,* &c. do not join readily with the preceding letter; and some cases in which a farther contraction is desirable, in order to increase the ease and rapidity of the writing. These cases are specified as follows:—

SPEC.—1. Where ⌒ follows | and |, and where ⌐ follows || \ and \, the circle is properly written on the right side of the || &c., as follows: ⌒ ⌐ ⌐

2. For the sake of contraction in some words of frequent occurrence the *r* may be omitted, and the circle written on the outside of the angle, as in \

extra,   obstruct.

REM. 1.—Whether this form of contraction can be safely adopted in any given case or not will depend partly upon the liability of confounding the contracted form with any other word of similar outline, and partly upon the frequency of the use of the contracted word. The words *prescribe* and *prescription*, for instance, may be contracted; and the words *proscribe* and *proscription* may be written more fully. Yet the usage would change in different departments of literary work, for the words that are of frequent occurrence in one department of literature or science may be very infrequent in another.

3. In some words where the trigraphs follow the curved letters, the circle will occur on the back of the curve. This use of the circle is not difficult where the curve ends in the direction of the added letter, as in

unstrung.

But where the added letter follows in a different direction, it is better to write the long , as in .

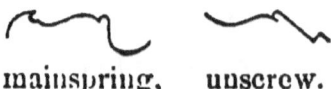

mainspring,   unscrew.

CHAPTER II.   49

4. Where the circle occurs on the inside of the curve, it is not necessary that the hook appear; but where it is convenient to make it, it will add to the perspicuity.

Examples.

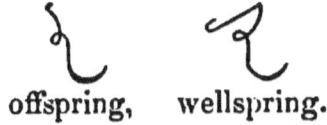

offspring,   wellspring.

5. The above principles will also apply to cases where ⌐\ and ⌐ are preceded by *s;* but the ⌒ may be freely used when convenience requires it.

REM.—In all cases of difficult joining with these trigraphs, where the above specifications do not apply, the fuller forms employed in the common style will be found to be always convenient and unobjectionable. The shortened forms are not *necessary,* but are employed merely for the sake of securing greater brevity; so where they do not aid the writer, there is no need that they should be employed to burden and complicate his style.

THE CIRCLE BEFORE ╱ ╱ AND ⌒.

17. *a.* In the commencement of a word, the circle is written on the under side of the ╱ for *sr,* and on the upper side for *sw.*

b. In the midst of a word, the hook of the ╱ must always appear; but the *sr* may be written with the hook on either side:—

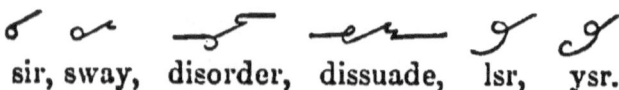
sir, sway, disorder, dissuade, lsr, ysr.

c. The circle may be written on the back side of the curve in such combinations as

msw, ssw.

d. Before ⌒, the ⌒ is most convenient in such words as *Soho, Sahara;* but the circle may be written in the hook without especial inconvenience.

In the word *falsehood,* the ⌒ is omitted.

§ BEFORE THE COMPOUNDS OF THE L-SERIES, AND J AND CHA.

18. *a.* Before the compounds ⌠ ⌠ ⌡ ⌡ and ⌡ initial *s* is written by the full sign ⌒, since this form is more easily written than the circle; but when another consonant precedes the *s,* it is frequently convenient to use the circle. Examples:—

sickly, exclaim.

b. The circle can be written in the hook of ⌒ ⌒ ⌡ ⌡ ⌒ (see sec. 26, *a*); but ⌒ ⌒

CHAPTER II.   51

come under the principle mentioned in the preceding paragraph.

Examples.

stl, sdl, s-shl, misjudge, mischief.

SPEC. — In cases where it is inconvenient to use the circle before these compounds in the midst of a word without some change of form, the writer may avoid the difficulty in the following ways: —

1. He may use the ⌒. This is always allowable, and is generally the best way where the following compound belongs to the initial series.

Examples.

misplace, discipline.

2. Other modes of overcoming this difficulty are allowable. *a.* The hook may be omitted, as in ↶ *explain;* or, *b.* The hook may be written after the circle, by means of a connecting stroke, as in ↷ *disclose.*

REM. 1. — Mr. Pitman authorizes another mode of writing the hooks of the L and R series after the circle in such cases as those specified above. It is that of making an imperfect hook where it cannot be perfectly formed. This can be done if the writer can afford to pause long enough to do it; but either of the methods recommended above is more consistent with speed in writing, and more likely to afford distinctly-legible word-forms.

REM. 2. — The *s* is never omitted, except in the case of word-signs. The circle is added to word-signs when they take the plural number, or any other modification containing this sound.

VOCALIZATION OF WORDS CONTAINING THE CIRCLE AND DOUBLE CIRCLE.

19. When disjoined vowels are used in words written with the circle or double circle, their position must be determined with reference to the full-sized letter to which the circle is attached: as, for instance, in the example previously given: The dot is read after the main stem, near which it is placed, and before the circle. But in the following words the circle is read first, and the vowel between it and the main stem:—

sup, sad, unsatisfied.

Spec. 1.—So, we have two cases. *a.* Where the circle is on the end of a stem, as shown in the former illustration. Here the vocal is written after the stem that precedes the circle. *b.* Where the circle is on the first of the stem. Here the vocal is written before the stem that follows the circle, as in the last illustration. Both cases are united in the word *unsatisfied.*

2. Observe, also, that letters preceding or following the stem to be vocalized do not affect the vocalization. In

the word *unsatisfied*, for instance, the syllable *un*, which precedes, and the syllable *fied* which follows, do not change the position which the vocals assume to the stem, *satis* (*sts*), which is to be vocalized.

REM. 1.—It must not be inferred that the vocal signs are to be frequently inserted. They may be omitted in most cases. Even the words *sup, sad,* and *unsatisfied*, which we have used as illustrations, are usually written without the vowels. Yet, it is sometimes necessary to insert a disjoined vocal for greater distinctiveness, and when used, it should be used in accordance with the principles here given.

REM. 2.—The general rules for writing the circle between two consonants are given in the Elements, page 71. These rules should be followed.

The rule most frequently violated is *Case* 3,—" Between a straight and a curved line, the circle is always on the *inside of the curve*." This, also, is illustrated in the word *unsatisfied*, as given above.

20. Stems with which double circles are connected are vocalized in the same manner as those which contain a single circle; but, in addition to this, the double circle admits, in some cases, an *inserted* vowel, which is read between the two *s*'s.

Examples.

analyses, cisalpine.

1. Since the double circle primarily represents *sus, ses, sez,* the vocals \ and · need not be inserted; and it is seldom necessary or expedient to insert the ⌒ or ⌒. Even

the words *analysis* and *analyses* will be sufficiently distinguished by shading or thickening the circle on one side to represent *sez*. The only object of inserting the vocal in such a case would be to designate the fact that the *e* in this syllable is long, which in ordinary writing would be unnecessary.

2. The other vocal signs, such as ⸴, ⊂, or v, may be inserted in the double circle in such words as *saucebox*, *exercising*. But these, and all other words, may be written more fully by means of the ⌒ or ⌢ and a single circle, if the writer chooses the longer form.

Rem.—Here, as in the case above, a mode of contraction is given to meet a few special cases; and the student should not press such forms into service on all possible occasions, but choose instead the plainer form, when such form is convenient for use.

CHAPTER II.

WRITING EXERCISE SECOND.

Apes, opes, adds, odds, aids, odes. Apace, apiece, apis. Base, bass, boss, bias. Case, kiss, chaos. Fuss, face, office. Pass, pace, piece, peace, pious.

Place, pulse, bless, bliss, blouse. Dross, dress, trace, trice, truce. Press, price, pierce, purse. Brace, Bruce, bourse. Grace, grass, grouse. Crease, cross, cress. Glass, gloss, glassy, glossy, dressy, drossy. Vase, vice, voice. Mace, mass, muss, mess, mice, mouse, moose. Nice, gneis, niece, noose.

Lace, lease, loose, loss, less, lass: Alas, Elias, alius, Lewis, Lucy. Race, racy, iris, rice, ruse. Chase, chess, choice. Fleece, floss.

Sip, sup, sop, sap, sick, suck, sock, sack, sake, seek, soak, set, sat, soot, sot. Seed, said, sowed, sawed, sad, sods, sighed, sued, sieve, save, salve, says, size, seize, sues.

Cease, sauce, siss, cess, souse, assess, recess, assessing, ceasing, tracing, gracing, racing, pressing.

Specify, spice, space, suppose, supper, superior, superfine, superficial, soporific, submissive, substantial, subsoil, suggesting, succeed, success, successful, unsuccessful. Satisfy, satisfied, unsatisfied, sudden, suddenly. Decency, citizen, citizenship. Situate, situated, settle, unsettled, sadly, Saturday, suffice, suffuse, sovereign, sovereignty, suffer, sufferance, insufferable, south, southern, seethe, seen, same, some, sum, assume, sameness, seeming, wholesome, unseemly. Soon, scene, sane, sign, saxon, sound, sown, unseen, unsound. Sing, sung, sang, singing, song, sing-song, sink, sank, sunk.

Seal, sail, soul, soil, sailing, soiling, unsealing, selling, sold, seldom, soldier.

Ask, acid, astonish, asp, assiduity, assiduous, associate, assign, assail, acerbity, aspen, asserted, assorted.

BRIEF SENTENCES CONTAINING THE WORDS GIVEN ABOVE.

If the price of the book you hav in press suits my purs, it is my purpos to purchas it. Messieurs Brace and Bruce wer at the Bourse. In pious mood they pas apace, and slowly pace in peace. He ads to the ods, and aids them with his odes. The base boss has a decided bias. In this case, what is a kis? Did he say case or chaos? In face of the foss, with much fuss, he announced his office. Bles the giver of blis. The grouse was in the gras, with grace in form and fether. Her glossy wing is dressy,—I do not say her glassy wing is drossy. This mas of mice have made a pretty mus. The loss of the lass is les on this lease than on the lace for her bridal array. Alas for Elias, alias Lewis and Luce! Too loose. Alas for Lucy! As he sowed the seed, he sighed (sihd), and sed how sad the sod! Let them cease to assess tiths on sauce and souse. Suppose we leave this space for spice, and specify some superior articles for use at supper. They sip and sup the sap. Som persons assume wholesom authority. Being requested to sing, she sung a song, and as she sang, a blush so soon, the sign of modesty, began to suffuse itself unseen over every feature. Let this suffice.

WRITING EXERCISE THIRD.

The Circle for Z, and the Double Circle.

His, has, does, these, use, was. Observe, observing,

observer, reserve, deserve, subserve, discern, reservoir, dissolve, resolve, Methodism, baptism, Catholicism. Reason, reasoning, unreasonable.

Long Sign, ⌒.

Zinc, zero, zany, zepher, zeal, zealous, zealot, zealously, zone, zoology, zion, zenith, season, seasonable, seasoning, business, emblazon, risen, rosin, rising, arisen, arising, reside, preside. Praising, prizing, pleasing, supposing, enclosing, disposing. Theism, deism, barbarism, fanaticism, Armenianism, agrarianism, Presbyterianism.

Circle for the Plural Number.

Advantages, advantageous, principles, represents, forms, objects, subjects, values, numbers, remarks, pleasures.

Miscellaneous Phrases.

These are, these things, has been, his time, his work, has led, does this, was it, was to, was sure, was seen, was done, was so, was present, was deceived, many days, many ways, he goes, his days.

The Double Circle.

Sustenance, sustaining, sesquitone, suspicious, unsuspicious, unsuspiciously, suspend. Necessary, necessarily, unnecessarily. Ancestor, ancestry, ancestral. Glances, trances, prances, glimpses, senses, essences, excrescences.

Miscellaneous.

Recess, recesses, races, reposes, imposes, ciceronian, thesis, theses, antithesis, antitheses, hypothesis, hypotheses, synthesis, syntheses, apotheosis, society, Cæsar, access, success, accessible, successful, successive, inaccessible, assisting, resisting.

Trigraphs.

Strive, streak, stratify, strategy, sprung, sprang, scream. Supper, sadder, sucker, screw, scribe, describe, disagree-

able, distress, disprove, disapprove, express, expressive, expressing, excrescence. Restrain, restore, respire, prosper, prosperous, unprosperous. Extraneous, extra, prescribe, proscribe, subscribe, superscribe, unstrung, down-stroke, mainspring, shoe-string, unscrew, offspring, wellspring. Surround, survive, reserve, disorder, sway, persuade, dissuade. Yes, sir; no, sir. Sahara, falsehood. So-sweet, may-sway. Exclude, exclaim, icicle, sick, sickly, suckle. Disciplinarian, misplacing, explanatory, unexplained, disclosing, disclaim, disciple, gospel. Expletive, explicit, explode, explore, explosive, expel, expulsion, extramundane, extrajudicial, extravagancy, extreme, extremely, extremity, extricable, extrinsic, extrude.

Miscellaneous.

Swiss, swindle, sepulcher, scissors. Suggestive, substantial, sublime, submissive, subscriber, substratum, substitute, subside, suffer, suffering, suffix, sufflate, sulphur, sultry, sun-stroke, sunrise, superabound, superadd, superfluous, superstratum, supersede, supervene, supply, supposable, suppleness, suppress, surprise, sustenance, suspend, satisfy, statistician, statesmanship.

> *Grasp the whole world of reason, life, and sense*
> *In one close system of benevolence:*
> *Happier, as kindlier, in whate'er degree,*
> *A hiht of blis is hiht of charity.*

> *As some tall clif that lifts its awful form,*
> *Swels from the vale, and midway leaves the storm,*
> *Tho' round its brest the rolling clouds are spred,*
> *Eternal sunshine settles on its hed.*

> *Deceit is the false road to happines,*
> *And all the joys we travel to thro' vice,*
> *Like fairy banquets, vanish when we touch them.*

CHAPTER III.

EXTENDED USE OF THE COMPOUNDS OF THE L AND R SERIES.

21. *a.* The principles of the Common style in regard to the use of the signs of the L and R series of compounds are followed largely in the Note-Taker's style. The use of these signs is, however, in this style extended somewhat. The omission of the vocals in some words renders the use of the compound sign convenient where it could not be used with the fully-vocalized forms.

Examples.—feeble, people, travel, drivel, gravel. (R. L. Sixth, 15.)

To these examples may be added many words containing these sounds, when they occur in unaccented syllables in the end of words of more than two syllables, as *musical, poetical, strategical, affable, suicidal, supernal, eternal, ambrosial,* &c. (R. L. Sixth, 15.)

b. There are, on the other hand, many cases in which the compound sign is inconvenient.

The full form should be written in these cases, because it is more convenient.

Examples.—*Able, table, rebel, durable, marble, fallible.* (R. L. Sixth, 16.)

c. The compound sign should not be used when a full vowel occurs between the *l* or *r* and the preceding *p, t, d,* or other consonant with which they unite. A few exceptions are, however, admitted for convenience' sake, as in the words

call, dear, full, sure, till.

It is not easy to give a general rule that will enable the writer to determine in every case whether to use the longer or shorter forms for words of the class treated of in this section. Indeed, it is not necessary that usage should be entirely uniform in this respect. Yet, as most persons will desire to secure all the brevity consistent with perfect legibility, the following suggestions and examples are added.

SPEC. 1.—In certain groups of words, a distinction of outline can be secured only by the use of vocals in some of the words of the group.

a. The *dtr* group comprises the words *debtor, doubter, deter, daughter, auditor, editor, auditory.* (For outlines see R. L. Sixth, 18, *a.*)

b. The *ttr* group comprises the words *tatter, tetter, titter, tighter, totter, tutor.*

c. Ppr.—*Peeper, pepper, paper, pauper, piper.*

d. Bbl.—*Babel, babble, Bible, bubble.*

CHAPTER III. 61

 e. Ttl.—*Tuttle, tittle, tottle, title.*
 f. Fble.—*Fable, feeble, foible, affable, effable.*
 g. Vl.—*Evil, oval, vale, vile, vial, valley, volley.* (R. L. Sixth, 18, *b, c, d, e, f, g.*)

 REM.—Other groups similar to the above may be given by the teacher, or selected by the student. These will suffice to illustrate the manner of distinguishing such words

 2. When *s* precedes syllables in which the *l* or *r* series of compounds may be used, the writer will adopt one of the three following modes of writing the words.
 a. The circle may be used, and the following compound separated into its elements as in the words

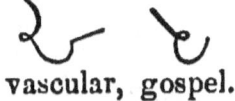

vascular, gospel.

 b. The ⁀ may be used followed by the hooked sign, as in

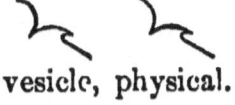

vesicle, physical.

 c. Where it can be done conveniently, the hook may follow the circle, as in the case of initial compounds treated of more specifically in the preceding chapter.

Examples.

Bristol, briskly.

REM. 1.—Examples under this case are not very numerous; and it will always be possible to substitute for these forms those given under case *b*. They may be distinguished, however, by the careful student. In these cases, *a* and *b*, either the hook or the circle must be sacrificed; hence the question will arise, which form of contraction is most natural, most legible, or most easily made?

By referring to the examples given, it will be observed that the words *vascular* and *gospel* do not properly demand the hooked signs. Neither is the circle *demanded* by any principle of the style. Since both forms of contraction are only tolerated in the examples mentioned for convenience. the question resolves itself into this, —which form is most convenient, the long ⌒, followed by the hooked letter, or the circle as given in the text?

The principal reason for preferring the circle here is because the resulting outlines are less *angular* than they would be with ⌒. (For further discussion of these principles, see the concluding chapter on Eugraphy.)

In the examples *vesicle* and *physical*, another principle enters. Though the same advantage would result from the use of the circle which we have pointed out in the former examples, yet there are two reasons for using the ⌒ and ⌒. 1st. The *s* is followed by a vowel. 2nd. The final syllable is a true compound (see Elements, page 75), and admits the sign properly, while in the case of *vascular* and *gospel* the use of the ⌒, ⌒ would be irregular.

We leave the student to apply the principle to other cases.

REM. 2.—Cases in which the hook may follow the circle need no special designation, for it is always allowable to use the circle and added hooked sign when it can be done conveniently, except in the cases mentioned in specification 1, where there are other words which might assume the same outline. In these cases, the word of most frequent occurrence is written with the briefest outline. (R. L. Sixth, 19.)

3. The following words, and some others, admit the vowel between the stem and the hook of the signs of the L and R hook series of compounds:—

Culture, with all the derivatives and compounds formed

from it, such as *agriculture, horticulture, uncultured, culprit, pilgrim, pilgrimage, philology, philosophy, telegraph, telegram, telescope.* (R. L. Seventh, 32, *a*.)

4. It is not necessary generally to vocalize those outlines which admit the vowel between the hook and the stem; but if, for any reason, it is desired, they may be vocalized in this manner:—

a. Semicircles may be written through the stem.

b. The dots may be made into a small circle, and placed after the stem to be vocalized.

c. The dashes may be struck through the stem when they are written in a direction at an angle with it, otherwise they may be placed after it. (For examples see R. L. Seventh, 32, *b*.)

THE USE OF ⟩ ⟩ FOR ⟨ ⟨.

22. The signs ⟩ and ⟩ are used to represent the sounds of *jr* and *chr* in such words as

Teacher, preacher, danger, larger.

This is in analogy with the use of (for ⌒ in the word-signs for *large* and *advantage*. (See table, Chapter I.)

SPEC. 1.— This form of contraction is not applied to many words in the Note-Taker's style, but only to a few words of frequent occurrence. The signs ⟩ and ⟩ must be preserved for their original use, as representing the sounds *zhr* and *shr* in all cases in which these sounds occur; but in cases where there would be no indefiniteness, the *jr* and *chr* may be so written.

2. The use of a vowel with these signs may be sufficient to make the outline perfectly legible, and this will be frequently convenient with the vowels ⌒, ⌒, ⁄, and others, as in the words *pitcher, preacher, teacher, voucher.*

With these words should be contrasted the normal use of these signs in such words as *measure, treasure, pressure,* &c. (R. L. Sixth, 20.)

THE USE OF ⊃ ⊃ OR ∪ ∪ FOR ⌐ ⌐.

23. *a.* The signs ⊃ ⊃ may be used for *jl* and *chl* in some words, as in

vigil, fragile.

b. The signs ∪ ∪ may be used instead of ⊃ ⊃ when they are more convenient, as in the words

angel, angelic.

SPEC.—The following words may be contracted in this way: *agile, agility, angel, angelic, bachelor, flagellate, fragile, fragility, vigil, vigilance.* (R. L. Sixth, 21.)

CHAPTER III.

WRITING EXERCISE FOURTH.

Babel, babble, bubble, Papal, people, pupil, pebble. Paper, pauper, pepper, piper, popper.
Auditor, auditory, daughter, debtor, doubter, deter. Tatter, tetter, titter, tighter, totter, tutor. Tattle, title, total, tittle.
Affable, fable, feeble, foible. Evil, oval, valley, volley, vile, viol. Awful, fail, fall, feel, fell, fill, file, fool, fowl, full, awfully, folly, foully, fully, fulfil.
Audible, edible, double, terrible, treble, trouble, drabble, durable. Travel, drivel, trifle, truffle. Frivolous, level, leveler, revel, revelers, revelry, civil, civilly. Novel, novelty, cavil, gravel, bevel.
Rider, reader, rudder, writer, rioter, wrecker, recur, harbor, harper, harsher, maker, meeker, seeker, sicker, secure, looker, locker, knocker.
Able, unable, enable, disable, ability, disability, rebel, rabble, ribaldry, marble, fallible, unavailable. Journey, journal. New Hampshire. CALL, DEAR, FULL, SURE, TILL, *until, surely, ensure. Gospel, expel, dispel, fiscal, vascular, vesicle, physical, Paschal, Bristol, briskly, musical. Rascal, muscular, vestal, festal, mustily, hastily. Fragile, fragility, flagellate, vigil, vigilance, frivolous, leveler, revelry, novelty, frivolity, philological. Phrenological, physiological, philosophical. Pilgrim, pilgrimage, telescope, telegram. Delaware.*

Brief Sentences comprising the above Words.

The daughter of an editor met a debtor. Auditor, said she, you may be a doubter, but this shall not deter me from appealing to a larger auditory. The tower of Babel, according to the Bible, was a great bubble, and ended in bubble. That pauper orderd pepper and paper, and the piper orderd a popper. That feeble but affable lady spoke of the young man's fable as a characteristic foible. He fell like a fool: how awful the fall! Words fail to give full emphasis to the foul folly, and awfully he has fulfilled an evil destiny.

For ill can poetry expres full meny a tone of tho't sublime,
And sculpture, mute and motionles, steals but one glans from time;
But by the wondrus actor's skil their weded triumphs com,—
Vers ceases to be airy tho't, and sculpture to be dum.

The Gift of Tungs.

When men had bin taut to look upon all men as brethren, then, and then only, did the variety of human speech present itself as a problem that calld for a solution in the eyes of tho'tful observers. I therefore date the real begining of the science of language from the day of Pentecost. After that day of cloven tungs, a new light is spreding over the earth, and objects rise into view which had bin hidden from the eyes of the nations of antiquity. Old words assume a new meaning, old problems a new interest, old sciences a new purpos. The comon origin of mankind, the diferences of race and language, the susceptibility of all nations to the hihest mental culture,— these become in the new world in which we live problems of scientific, because of more than scientific, interest.

MAX MUELLER.

CHAPTER III.

THE PREFIXES AB, AP, AG, AC, AD, AND AT OMITTED.

24. *a*. In such words as *abbreviate* and *approximate* the *ab* and *ap* may be omitted, writing *breviate, proximate*.

Ex.— ⌡ *abbreviate*.

So *ag* and *ac*, *ad* and *at*, where followed by *gr*, *cr*, *dr*, and *tr* may be omitted.

Ex.—*Address, attribute, aggress, accredit*, written *dress, tribute, gress, credit*.

b. The prefixes *ac, af*, and *ag* may in like manner be omitted in some cases before *cl, fl*, and *gl*, as in *acclimate, afflict, agglutinate*, written *climate, flict, glutinate*.

Spec. 1.—The number of words containing these prefixes is small, and the student should fix upon definite outlines for each.

Those omitting the prefix are *abbreviate, accredit, accrue, address, aggrandize, aggress, appreciate, appropriate, approximate, attract, attribute*, and their derivitives. (R. L. Seventh, 24, *a*.) *Acclimate, acclivity, afflatus, afflict, affluence, agglomerate, agglutinate*, and their derivatives. (R. L. Seventh, 24, *b*.)

2. In a few cases the prefix is written, and the following *g* or *p* omitted, as in ⌐⌐, *apprehensive*.

The words which follow this mode are *aggregate, ag-*

grieve, appropriate, approach, approve, apply, and their derivatives. (R. L. Seventh, 24, *c.*)

Rem. — Other forms of contraction not yet explained enter into the formation of the outlines of some of the words given in this section; and they are on this account omitted from the reading lesson (Lesson Seventh), but they are given in the vocabulary.

3. In some cases, both the prefix and the following consonant may be written, as ⌇, *acclaim.*

This will be necessary only when the contracted form would be liable to be confounded with the word stripped of the prefix, and in the case, for the most part, of words of infrequent occurrence, such as *afflux, appraise,* which might be confounded with *flux* and *praise.* (R. L. Seventh, 24, *d.*)

Rem. 1. — The examples given in Spec. 2 also distinguish the words so contracted from the root-word, or some other word of similar outline. In this way, *approve* is distinguished from *prove, aggrieve* from *grieve,* and *approach* from *preach.*

Rem. 2. — It is not necessary that all such words should be distinguished by difference of outline. In many cases the word-form will be rendered definite by the use of the words in a sentence, although capable of two meanings when standing alone. This is the case when one of the words is a noun or adjective only, and the other a verb, as in the case of the words *tribute* and *attribute, proximate* and *approximate.*

But though both words designated by a given outline are of the same part of speech, there may be still some peculiarity of use that will clearly distinguish them in a sentence, as in the case of *dress* and *address.*

THE PREFIX AD BEFORE V AND J.

25. *a.* Where the prefix *ad* is followed by *v*, as in the words *adverb, advise,* the — may be omitted, and the vowel ʊ may be written for *ad*.

SPEC. 1. — The word *advantage,* and all its derivatives, are written with contracted forms, as given in the tables of word-signs. (R. L. Seventh, 25, *b*.)

2. The words *adverse, adversity, adverseness,* and *adversely* may be written ⌒↩, &c., to distinguish them from *averse* and its derivatives. (R. L. Seventh, 26, *a* and *b*.)

b. The vocal ʊ may also be written for *ad* when this prefix is followed by *j*, as in the words *adjoin, adjust,* written ⌒↶   ⌒↪.

SPEC. — In this manner may be written the words *adjudge, adjure, adjoin, adjust, adjutor,* and their derivatives (R. L. Seventh, 27) and *adject, adjacent, adjudicate, adjunct, adjuvant,* and their derivatives.

WRITING EXERCISE FIFTH.

Abbreviate, accrue, attribute, address, aggress, aggressor, acclivity, afflatus, affluence, approximation, agglomeration, aggrieve, aggrievance, appropriate, approach, approachable, approaching, unapproachable, aggravate, aggravated, approve, approvable, apply, applicable, unapplied, afflux, applause, appraise, apprise, applaud.

Advance, advantage, advise, adviser, advisory, advocacy, advowson, adverb, adversary, adversative, adversity, advice, averse, aversely, adjacency, adjoin, adjudge, adjure, adjurer, adjust, adjustable, adjusting.

Brief Sentences containing some of the above Words.

Appearances ar ofen deceitful. They approov the desine, and wil endevor to proov its superior merits. They praise the work, and appraise the value of the labor at one thousand dollars. I am sure they wil please and gain applause. He was addrest as the aggressor, and was greatly aggrievd by the implied censure. He was averse to these adverse mesures. They preach an approaching doom. We advise an advance.

Kepler's Prayer.

Thou who by the liht of nature hast kindld in us the longing after the liht of thy Grace, in order to raise us to the liht of Thy Glory, thanks to thee, Creator and Lord, that Thou lettest me rejoice in Thy works. Lo, I hav don the work of my life with that power of intelect which Thou hast given. I hav recorded to men the glory of Thy works as far as my mind cud comprehend their infinit majesty. * * If, by the wonderful buty of Thy works, I hav bin led into boldnes, if I hav saut my own honor among men as I advanst in the work which was destind to Thine honor, pardon me in kindness and charity, and, by Thy Grace, grant that my teaching may be to Thy glory and the welfare of all men. Praise ye the Lord, ye hevenly harmonies; and ye that understand the new harmonies, praise the Lord — KEPLER'S HARMONY OF THE WORLD.

CHAPTER III.

BRIEFER SIGNS FOR QUA AND GUA.

26. *a.* A new sign is made to represent the sound of *qu* in *queen*, ⌒, named *qua*. It resembles ⌒, but has a larger hook. It differs from the ⌒ (*wha*) in that the latter has a smaller, *heavy* hook, while the ⌒ (*qua*) has a larger, *light* hook.

b. This sign is used for *qu* quite generally, as in the words

quench, qualify.

c. The full form is used in some words containing *qu* for the purpose of securing outlines more easily vocalized, or word-forms more convenient, as in

equal, obsequeous.

SPEC. 1.—The ⌒ is used in the following words: *quiet, quality, quarrel, quarters, quarto. Unqualified, unquenchable, request,* &c.

SPEC. 2.—The ⌒ is used for *qu* in all cases except the following: the full form is written—

a. Where the *qu* is preceded by *c*, as in *acquire, acquiesce.*

b. Where any vowel precedes the *qu* that is joined more easily to the ╲ than to the ╱, as in *equal, equanimity.*

c. In some cases, where the circle precedes the *qu*, especially in the midst of the word, as in *obsequious, sequel.*

d. Where the *q* is under accent, and separated from the *u* in pronunciation, as in *equity, requisite.* (R. L. Seventh, 28, *b.*)

Rem.—For other examples, see Writing Exercise Sixth.

27. The hook of the ╱ is made heavier, thus ╱, to provide a sign for *gua* in such words as *languid, lingual.*

Spec.—This sign is employed in only a few words, such as *sanguine, linguist, languish*, with the words derived from them, and a few others. (R. L. Seventh, 29.)

Rem.—The compound sounds *dw, tw,* and *thw* are written with ─╱ ─╱ ╲╱, as in the first style of the art.

CONTRACTED SIGNS FOR HA AND WHA.

28. *a.* The stem of ╱ is dropped before ⌒ in some words, as in ⌒ *him* or *home.*

b. The stem of ╱ is also dropped before ╱ in the words *whole* and *health*, and their derivatives, and before ─,),), and ╲ in the words

─   )   )   ╲

head, heavy, half, hath,

and their derivatives and compounds.

CHAPTER III. 73

Spec. 1.— The stem of the ╱ is dropped before ⌒ in the word *home* and its derivatives and compounds, *homely, homebred,* &c., and in the words *hamper, human, humble, humility, humor,* and their derivatives. (R. L. Seventh, 30, *a.*)

Spec. 2. — The principal derivatives from the words *whole, health, head,* and *heavy* are *wholly, wholesome, unwholesome, wholesale, healthful, healthy, healthiness; heady, headless, headstone, heavily, heavy-laden, half-length.* (R. L. Seventh, 30, *b.*)

29. *a.* The stem of ╱ is omitted before ⌒ and ⌒ in the word ⌒, *whim,* and its derivatives, and in *while* and *whelm.*

b. The stem of ╱ is also omitted before ⌣ in the word-sign *when,* and the ╱ is entirely dropped from the words ⌒, *overwhelm,* and ⌒, *elsewhere.*

Spec.— Connected with *whim* are the words *whimsical, whimsically,* and *whimper.* With *when* we have *whence, whenever, whensoever;* and with *while, whilst, whelm,* and *whelming.* (R. L. Seventh, 31.)

WRITING EXERCISE SIXTH.

Quick, quiet, quarrel, quench, quill, quail, quart, query, quarry, quintuple, quadruped, quaff, qualify, quality, quandary, quantity, quarto, quartz, querulous, quib, quickness, quiesce, quiescence, quietism, quietly, quietness, quietude, quietus, quire, quiz, quizzical, quizzing, quo animo, *quota, quoth, quotidian,* quo warranto.

Equal, aqueous, aquafortis, equality, equiform, equiformity, equip, equipage, equipoise. Acquire, acquiring, equity, acquiesce, aqueduct, obsequious.

Languid, lingual, sanguine, languish, linguist. Him, homely, hamper, humor, humorous, humorously, human, humble, humility. Whole, wholly, wholesome, wholesomeness, wholesale. Health, healthful, healthy, healthfulness, healthiness. Whim, whimsical, whimper, whelm, overwhelm, overwhelming, elsewhere, while, whilst. Heavy, heavier, heavily, half, hath.

Brief Sentences containing some of the above Words.

They wil quickly quench the fires of discord. They wil acquire a quantity of queer quails quils. With quizical inquiries and querulous language, they accepted the equipage. They acquiesce obsequiously in the equity of this iniquitous mesure. We object to the quality not to the quantity of the quarts from that quarry. In his linguistic harang, he sed he was sanguin of succes. His humbl home did not hamper his genius. His humor is wholesome, tho' often whimsical. To him that hath shal be given. While they wer assembling an overwhelming force, the veterans wer laboring elsewhere without a whimper.

CHAPTER III.

Miscellaneous.

*Knolege dwels
In heds replete with tho'ts of other men;
Wisdom, in minds attentiv to their own.*

*Ask for what end the hevenly bodies shine?
Erth for whose use? Man anscrs 'Tis for mine:
For me kind Nature wakes her genial power,
Suckles each herb, and spreds out every flower;
Annual for me the grape, the rose, renew,
The juce nectareus, and the bamy dew;
For me helth gushes from a thousand springs;
For me the mine a thousand tresures brings,
Seas roll to waft me, suns to light me rise,—
My foot-stool, erth, my canopy, the skies.*

To promote an unworthy person disgraces humanity. Humility is that low, sweet root from which all hevenly virtues shoot. He that aims at the sun wil not hit it, but his arro wil fly hiher than if he aimed at an object on a level with himself.

WRITING EXERCISE SIXTH.— PART SECOND.

THE STREAM OF LIFE—*Life bears us on like the stream of a mihty river. Our boat at first glides down the narrow channel, throo the playful murmurings of the little brook, and the windings of its grassy border. The trees shed their blossoms over our young heds; the flowers on the brink seem to offer themselves to our young hands; we ar happy in hope; and we grasp egerly at the buties around us; but the stream hurries us on, and stil our hands are empty.*

Our cours in youth and manhood is along a wider and

deeper flood, and amid objects more striking and gorgeus. We ar animated by the mooving panorama of industry and plesure which passes before us; we ar excited by som petty success, or deprest and made miserable by some equally petty failure. But our energy and our dependence ar both in vain. The stream bears us on; and our joys and our griefs ar alike left behind us. Whether ruf or smooth, the river hasens towards its home, till the roaring of the ocean is in our ears, and the tossing of the waves is beneath our keel. The fields and hils disappear from before our eyes; the floods ar lifted up around us; and the erth looses sight of us. We take our last leav of the erth, and of its inhabitants, and of our further voyage there is no witnes but the Infinite and the Eternal.

CONTENTED AT NO AGE IN LIFE.

Laid in my quiet bed, in study as I wer,
I saw within my trubled hed a heap of tho'ts appear;
And every tho't did show so lively in mine eyes
That now I sihd, and then I smiled, as cause of tho'ts did rise.
I saw the little boy, in tho't how oft that he
Did wish of God to scape the rod, a tall young man to be.
The yung man eke, that feels his bones with pains opprest,
How he wud be a rich old man, to liv and lie at rest.
The rich old man that sees his end draw on so sore,
How he wud be a boy agen, to liv so much the more.
Wherat full oft I smiled to see how all these three,
From boy to man, from man to boy, wud chop and change degree.
And musing thus, I think the case is very strange
That man from welth to liv in wo doth ever seek to change.
EARL OF SURREY, about 1540.

CHAPTER IV.

HALF-LENGTH CHARACTERS.

30. *a.* In analogy with the final syllables of the *s* and *z* series, as given in the Elements, page 78, we have *d* and *t* uniting with a preceding consonant, as in the syllables *ant, ent, and, end.*

These syllables are contracted by writing the consonant sign that precedes the *d* or *t* half its usual length, thus implying the *d* or *t.*

b. This form of contraction properly applies in all cases where the sound of *d* or *t* unites with a preceding consonant, without any intervening vocal, as in the words

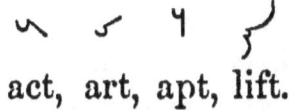

act, art, apt, lift.

SPEC. — It will be observed that a silent vowel is often written in the ordinary orthography between the *d* or *t* and the preceding consonant. As all silent vowels are disregarded in Tachygraphy, these syllables are treated as though no vowel occurred, as in the words ⁓, *lagged,* ⁓, *received.*

31. As in the case of the *s* and *z* series of final compounds, *s* united only with light signs, and

z only with heavy signs, so here light signs only are halved to imply *t*, and heavy signs to imply *d*.

SPEC. 1.—In accordance with a law of language that is nearly universal, only sounds that are similar in their degree of *hardness* can combine or blend together. The *t*, for instance, combines with the letters *p*, *k* (or *c*), *f*, *sh*, and *s;* and *d*, with *b*, *g*, *v*, *zh*, and *z;* and since in Tachygraphy light signs represent one class of sounds, and heavy signs another, it follows in practice that the sound of *t* combines only with light signs, and the sound of *d* only with heavy signs, except in the case of the liquids mentioned below.

2. The use of the shortened forms will be understood from the following examples, as given in Reading Lesson Eighth, 34:—

Act, apt, aft, left, lacked, lagged, lift, lived, hushed, breathed, wreathed, wished, ceased, seized, sect, supped, saved, received, soft, exist, diseased, deceased, lathed, lashed.

REM.—It should be observed that the verbal ending *ed* frequently sounds like *t*, and is added by halving the light signs, as in the words *lathed, lashed,* and others given above.

THE LIQUIDS.

32. *a.* The letters ⌒, ⌣, ╱, and ╱, though light, represent sounds that are variable in their quality. They unite readily with either light or heavy sounds, taking the *s* or *z*, *t* or *d*, into

CHAPTER IV. 79

combination with them. So these four letters are halved to represent both *d* and *t* after them.

b. When ⌒, ⌣, ⌐, or ╱ are halved to imply *d*, the halved letter is made heavy; but when halved to imply *t*, they remain light.

Examples.

aimed, end, willed, card, ant, wilt, cart.

REM.—The student of the art should be careful to limit this use of the liquids entirely to the four letters specified. The practice of making (, ⌢, or) heavy to imply *d* is an error.

ING AND OTHER LETTERS NOT SHORTENED.

33. *a.* The letter ⌣ is not shortened. If it were halved, it would be confounded with the shortened ⌣ when made heavy to imply *d*.

b. The letters ⎯, ⎯, used according to the principles of the preceding sections, are not halved to imply *t* or *d*, as it is easier in rapid writing to lengthen than to shorten horizontal strokes. Hence, such words as *arched, etched, edged, judged,* &c. are written in full. (R. L. Eighth, 36.)

c. The letters — and — do not unite with a

following *d* or *t* without an intervening vocal, and for this reason are not halved to express such union.

34. The shortened forms are used where convenient with great freedom, but there are some cases in which they cannot be used, and other cases in which the longer form is more convenient and distinctive. As these principles are important, they are discussed in separate sections.

SHORTENED LETTERS JOINED WITH FULL-SIZED LETTERS.

35. When halved letters are joined to full-sized letters, they must form a distinct angle. Where an angle cannot be formed, the letters must be written in full, as in

dealt, melt.

Spec.—An angle may be formed by means of a *hook*, vocal sign, or circle, as in the words *tilt, band, pained, present, crescent*. (R. L. Eighth, 37.)

36. Where the diphthong *ow* precedes *nd* and *nt* in such words as *sound, mount*, the ⌣ and

⌣ are written without contraction, and the vocal sign is omitted.

Examples.

bound, count, sound.

Spec. 1.—This is in accordance with a principle of the science that should be kept in remembrance, viz.: that *a diphthong or two vocals demand the full form of the consonant both before and after them;* but it should be observed that, since the vowel does not occur in these cases between the two characters united, but only *before* them, the necessity of using the full form of the consonant outline is not imperative.

2. Where the vowel is written, the half-length may follow it freely; but the question will still occur whether the full form with the vocal sign omitted is briefer and better than the shortened form with the vocal. Generally, the v is contracted before ⌣, and the ⁊ is omitted, as in *kind, fined, signed, mind, bind, found, mound, bound.* (R. L. Eighth, 38.)

37. Where a vowel follows the *d* or *t* in the end of a word, the full sign is written, as in

lofty, hasty, hardy.

Spec. 1.—This rule may be applied in the Note-Taker's style also to the derivatives of words of this class, as *lofty, loftiness, loftily, haughty, haughtier, haughtily, haughtiness, hasty, hastily.* (R. L. Eighth, 39.)

2. On the contrary, the derivatives of words ending in a shortened letter generally retain the shortened letter, as *effect, effective, restrict, restrictive, accept, acceptable.* (R. L. Eighth, 40.)

38. The half-length principle applies also to many words similar to those given in the preceding section, although not derived from words in which the shortened forms occur: such words are

article, particle, opportunity, practical.

SPEC. 1.—It is not necessary to enumerate the words that come under this class. They are numerous and varied in form and length, but they all have a common resemblance in one respect. They all contain a *t* or *d* preceded immediately by another consonant, with which it may unite, as *pract* in the word *practical, art* in *article,* and *port* in *opportunity.*

The following will serve as additional examples: *ordinary, pertinent, absurdity, rectify, fortify, fortitude, susceptible.* (R. L. Eighth, 41.)

REM.—In many of these cases the contracted letters are divided in pronunciation so as to stand in contiguous syllables, as in the examples just given, where *par-ti-cal* is written as though pronounced *part-ic-al.*

2. This principle is further extended to include words in which the *d* or *t* is separated by a vowel from the letter

with which it is contracted, as in the words *imperative, narrative*. These words are written by elision, as though pronounced *impertive, nartive*, and so resemble those given in Spec. 1. Other words of three or more syllables omit the unaccented vowel, and admit of this form of contraction, such as *operative, authoritative, primative, diminutive, equitable*. (R. L. Eighth, 42.)

3. This principle is still further extended to some words in which the vowel preceding the *t* is accented, as in *theoretical, dramatical, arithmetical, critical*. (R. L. Eighth, 43.)

REM.—In long words, the half-length principle can be applied with much more freedom than in short words. It will not, however, be necessary for the writer of the Note-Taker's style to burden himself much with contractions of this kind. The principle use of these shortened forms outside of a few words of frequent occurrence is in cases where an obtuse angle or a bad word-form may be avoided in this way, as in the words *practical, article, opportunity*, &c., given above.

EST AND STE CONTRASTED.

39. The diphthong *st* in the end of syllables comes under two modes of contraction, and may be written either with ⌒ or ⌒.

a. The ⌒ is used generally in cases where the circle would be used if not followed by *t*, as, for instance, the circle is used in *muss, less*, and *class*, so, the ⌒ is used in the analogous words *must, lest*, and *classed*. But where the

⌒ is employed in the primative word, the added *t* is indicated by making the ⌒ half-length, as in *cross, crossed, trace, traced.* (R. L. Fourteenth, 106, *a.*)

b. So, also, where the *st* is preceded by any full vowel or diphthong that would require an ⌒, in accordance with the rules for the circle, the ⌒ is employed, as in

post, coast.

40. As the *est* is contrasted with *ste* so ⌒ (*sest*) is sometimes written where *sus-te* would be an equally natural character.

a. The *sest* is preferred in the words

system, exist, subsist, possest,

and some other words.

b. The *sus-te* is used in *sustain, exhaust, incest,* and some other words.

Spec. 1.—The principal derivatives from the words *system, exist,* &c. are *systemize, systematic, unsystematic, existing, existence, existent, subsisting,* &c., which are written by adding the terminations to the forms given above.

2. The letters *s-st* may also be written ⌒. This form

will occur in the words *sowest, seest, sawest,* and wherever the *s*'s are separated by a diphthong or two vowel sounds.

3. The forms ⌒— and ⌢— will be understood from the explanations given in Chapter II, as they come under the principles given for the use of the circle.

EXCEPTIONAL FORMS.

41. *a.* The use of the half-length principle is extended in the EASY-REPORTING style to cases where a vowel occurs between the *d* and *t* and the preceding consonant, as in *might, night.* A few words of frequent occurrence may be so contracted in this style. We instance the following: *might, right, not, what, quite.* (R. L. Eighth, 44, *a.*)

b. To these may be added the following exceptional contractions, which imply a *d* by halving a light character, or *vice versa*, contrary to the general rule: *could, would, should, had, but, that, great.* (R. L. Eighth, 44, *b.*)

SPEC.—This list of exceptions should not be extended in case of short words. The rule which requires that *t* be implied only by shortening light signs, and *d* by shortening heavy signs, should be steadily kept in view.

c. Another class of exceptional forms consists

of words in which the compound signs of the L or R series, used irregularly (see Chapter III), are shortened to imply a *t* or *d*, as in the words ⁊ *short*, ⊂ *called*.

Spec.—The words so contracted are *short, shorten*, and derivatives, *short-hand, culture, cultivate*, and derivatives. (R. L. Eighth, 45.)

CHAPTER IV.

WRITING EXERCISE SEVENTH.

Apt, act, aft, rift, sift, swift. Tucked, lacked, lapped, picked, hushed, lagged, lived. Ant, end, cant, tend, wilt, willed, tilt, tilled, rent, rend, cart, card, tempt, hemmed. Except, expect, extinct, left, bereft, reflect, fact, distant, innocent, dependent, student, malignant, regained, hand. Lost, traced, post, toast, least, lowest, crossed. Band, sand, sinned, bard, hard, feared, soared, roamed, stemmed, mild, build, chilled, drilled, scanned, brand, grand.

Use the full forms in the following Words.

Arched, scorched, gaged, edged, etched, murdered.

Found, pound, round, fount, hasty, mighty, plenty, lofty.

Bend, spent, melt, dealt, cold, mold, sold. Kent, reckoned, second.

Contract V in the following Words.

Find, signed, resigned, declined, kind, bind, mind, designed, refined.

GOLD.

*Many hunted, swet, and bled for gold,
Waikt all the niht, and labord all the day.
And what was this allurement, dost thou ask?
A dust dug from the bowels of the erth,
Which, being cast into the fire, came out
A shining thing that fools admired, and calld
A god; and in devout and humble pliht
Before it neeld, — the greater to the les;
And on its altar sacrifized ease, peace,
Truth, faith, integrity, good concience, frends,
Love, charity, benevolence, and all*

> *The sweet and tender sympathies of life:*
> *And, to complete the horrid murderus rite,*
> *And signalize their folly, offered up*
> *Their souls, and an eternity of blis,—*
> *To gain them what?—an hour of dreaming joy.*
> *A feverish hour that hasted to be done,*
> *And ended in the bitternes of wo.*

ANECDOTE.—*One day, when the Moon was under an eclipse, she complained thus to the Sun for the discontinuance of his favor. "My dearest friend," said she, "why do you not shine upon me as you used to do?" "Do I not shine upon thee?" said the Sun. "I am very sure I intend to." "Oh, no," replied the Moon; "but now I see the reason; that dirty planet, the Earth, has got between us."*

WORKING A PASSAGE.—*An Irishman having applied to work his passage on a canal-boat, and being employed to lead the horses on the tow-path, on arriving at the end of his journey, declard he woud sooner go on foot than work his passage in Amerika.*

> *Who friendship with a knave has made*
> *Is judged a partner in the trade:*
> *'Tis thus that on the choice of frends*
> *Our good or evil name depends.*

WRITING EXERCISE EIGHTH.

Must, most, mist, mast, mused, amazed, amused. Lest, lost, lust, lowest, least, laced. Rest, rust, roast, roused. Zest, tust, tacit, toast, tyest, tossed. Crossed, crest, crust, crossed. Coast, kissed, cast, cost. Guest, ghost, gust. Trust, tryst, traced, truest, tryest.

CHAPTER IV. 89

Might, right, not, what, had, would, should, could, but, that.

Subordinate, importunity, opportunity, article, particle, practical. Effective, elective, ordinary, operative, authoritative, primitive, theoretical, dramatical, arithmetical. Eclectic, attractive, distracting, restrictive, destructive, critical, political.

Short, shorten, shorter, called, cultivate, uncultivated, culture, agriculture, horticulture.

System, systemize, systematic, unsystematic, subsisting, existing, existent, nonexistent. Exhausted, exhaustive, existences.

> *A cloud lay cradled near the setting sun:*
> *A gleam of crimson tinged its braided sno.*
> *Long had I watcht the glory mooving on*
> *O'er the stil radius of the lake belo.*
> *Tranquil its spirit seemd, and floated slo:*
> *E'en in its very motion there was rest,*
> *While every breth of eve that chanst to blo*
> *Wafted the traveler to the buteus west.*
> *Emblem, metho't of the departed soul,*
> *To hooz white robe the gleam of bliss is given,*
> *And by the breth of mercy made to roll*
> *Riht onward to the golden gates of heaven,*
> *Where, to the eye of faith, it peacful liez,*
> *And telz to man his glorius destiniz.*

OSSIAN'S ADDRESS TO THE MOON.—*Dauter of Heven, fair art thou! The silens of thy face iz plesant! Thou comest forth in lovlines. The stars attend thy blu cours in the east. The clouds rejois in thy presens, O Moon! They brighten their dark-brown sides. Who is like to thee in the hevens, liht of the silent niht? The stars in thy presens turn away their sparkling eyes. Whither dost thou retire from thy cours when the darknes of thy countenans groez? Hast thou thy hall like Ossian? Dwelest thou in the shado of grief? Hav thy sisters fallen from Heven? Ar they who rejoice with thee at niht no more? Yes, they hav fallen, fair liht, and thou dost often retire to mourn. But thou thyself shalt fail one niht, and leav thy blu path in Heven.*

Where wast thou when I laid the foundations of the erth? Or who laid the corner-stone thereof when the morning stars sang together, and all the sons of God shouted for joy? Hast thou commanded the morning since thy dayz, and causd the day-spring to know his place, that it miht take hold of the ends of the erth, that the wicked miht be shaken out of it? Hast thou perceivd the bredth of the erth? Declare if thou knowest it all! Where is the way where liht dwelleth? and as for darkness, where is the place thereof, that thou shouldst take it to the bound thereof, and that thou shouldst kno the paths to the house thereof? Knoest thou it because thou wast then born? or because the number of thy days is great?—JOB.

CHAPTER V.

LENGTHENED CURVES.

42. The consonant curves are made twice their usual length to imply the addition of *tr* or *dr* to their own proper sounds. This contraction applies properly, in the first instance, to cases in which *tr* follows the lengthened letter, without an intervening vowel, as in the words

after, enter, filter.

SPEC.—As the letters), (, ⌒, ⌐ do not unite with a following *dr* in this manner, this principle is not applied to them in its first use, but nearly all the light curves furnish examples, as in the following words: *laughter, rafter, disaster, boaster, foster, tempter (temter), winter, banter, falter.* (R. L. Ninth, 47.)

43. The doubled curves are farther used when a vowel intervenes between the lengthened letter and the added *tr* or *dr*, as in the words *letter, latter.*

SPEC. 1.—This principle also applies in practice only to the light curves.

Ex.—Fetter, fitter, shutter, shatter, litter, loiter, lighter, meter, matter, mutter. (R. L. Ninth, 48.)

2. The curves ⟩ and ⟫, and the light curves of the S-series initial, are doubled in the same manner as the simple letters.

Ex.— Fretter, fritter, flatter, flutter, slaughter, center, shelter. (R. L. Ninth, 49.)

44. The liquid curves ⌣ and ⟫, when doubled to imply *dr*, are made heavy, as ⌣ *under*, ⟫ *elder*.

SPEC. 1.—The following words will serve as illustrations of the use of these letters: *sunder, understand, underground, wonder, thunder, kinder, reminder, wilder, wilderness, bewilder.* (R. L. Ninth, 50.)

2. The letters ⌒ and ⌣ are not doubled to imply *dr*.

REM.—It will be observed that the *dr* and *tr*, when implied by the double-length curves, have no vowel between the *d* and *r*, or the *t* and *r*, but are pronounced as in the final syllables of *enter, fetter,* and *under*. It would not do, for instance, to use the double-length in *entire*, much less in *Ontario*. So, also, the word *lottery*, having a vowel after the *r*, is excluded from this class of contracts; but when another consonant is added, as in *lateral*, the principle will apply once more. (See also 45, *c*.)

45. *a*. The doubled curves may be vocalized in the same manner as the simple letters, but the connected vocals, if final, are read before the added letters, as in the word *latter*, given in section 42.

b. When the circle is added to a lengthened

curve, however, it is read last of all, as in letters, matters.

c. Other letters may follow the lengthened curve, as in the words *latterly, literal, elderly, flatterer, flattering, wondering.* (R. L. Ninth, 51.)

DR AND TR FOLLOWED BY A VOWEL.

46. When a vowel follows the *dr* and *tr*, as in the words *entry, sundry,* &c., the compounds of the R series are employed, as in the common style. This forms a convenient distinction between the forms of such words as *enter* and *entry, winter* and *wintry, sunder* and *sundry,* and others. (R. L. Ninth, 52. See also 44, Rem.)

47. Since many of the words which imply the *tr* and *dr* are such as might with propriety imply the *t* and *d* by means of the half-length characters, there is sometimes a conflict in the use of these two modes of contraction. Thus the forms *rend-er* and *render* are equally correct. The first form, however, is appropriate to the noun *render* (one who rends), as derived from *rend,* and the second form to the verb *render.*

Spec. 1.—It will not be necessary to enter minutely into distinctions of this kind. As a general rule, the double-length form will take the precedence of the half-length with the added *r*, on account of its greater brevity, where the use of either form is admissible.

2. The half-length takes the precedence of the double-length principle of contraction:—

a. In derivative words in which *er* is added to a word-form which ends in a halved letter, as in the case of *rend-er*, given above. Other examples are *soft, softer; round, rounder; haunt, haunter.*

b. So, also, in some cases where the preceding *nd* is uncontracted, as in *round, rounder.* (R. L. Ninth, 53.)

3. The choice between these modes of contraction gives opportunity for distinction of words, as ⌒ *hunter*, ⌒ *haunter*. But, on the other hand, we write

bind, binder, bindery, found, founder, foundry.

4. The ⌒ in *counter* is contracted, thus ⌒. This form is retained in *encounter*, and all derivatives and compounds, such as *countersign, counter-work*, &c. (R. L. Ninth, 54.)

THE SHORTENED ⌒ AND THE CIRCLE.

48. The trigraph *str* is written in several ways, some of which have been explained in Chapter II. These letters come under the lengthening

principle only where preceded by a vowel, and when no vowel follows them. Where either the *st* or *tr* form an initial compound, the signs of the *s* or *r* series of compounds must be used.

Where the *st* forms a final compound, four constructions are possible: *a* ⁔, *b* ⌒, *c* ⌢, *d* ⌣.

a. The use of the circle is restricted here in accordance with the principles taught in Chapter II, sections 9 to 13. As we use the circle in *pest,* so we use it in *pester* and *fester;* so, also, in *lustre, bluster,* &c. (R. L. Ninth, 55, *a.*)

b. The ⌒ is used in *muster, duster, jester, setter,* but the ⌢ is used in *suitor.* (R. L. Ninth, 55, *b.*)

c. Where *r* is added to a word in which the ⌒ is used, ⌢ is substituted for it. As we write *post* ⌊, *coast* ⌐, so we write ⌊⌢ *poster,* ⌐⌢ *coaster.* The use of the ⌢ will be determined by nearly the same considerations as are mentioned in Chapter IV, section 40, in regard to the ⌒.

SPEC.—*Ester* ⌢ is used in such words as *sister, cloister, blister, foster, Zoroaster, Lancaster, moister.* (R. L. Ninth, 55, *c.*)

d. The form ⌣ is seldom used.

ANGLES WITH LENGTHENED CURVES.

49. Lengthened curves cannot unite with other consonants without an angle. This is in accordance with a principle everywhere observed. When two consonant letters unite without an angle, they are understood to be of the same length.

Spec. 1.—The reason of this rule will be easily understood. The length of a letter cannot be determined unless its commencement and end are known.

2. The intervention of a vocal sign, or hook, or circle is sufficient to separate letters of different lengths. Some examples of this kind have already been given, as *kinder*, *binder* (so, also, the half-length, *bind* and *kind*), *banter*, *counter* (and *count*), *disaster*, *Zoroaster*. (R. L. Ninth, 47, 50, 54, and 55.)

EN AND ING TREBLED.

50. The letter ⌣ is made three times its usual length to imply the sounds of *thr* in the words ⌣‾‾‾ *another*, ‾‾‾‾ *neither*. This sign should be made light throughout, and will thus be distinguished from the forms given in the next section.

CHAPTER V. 97

Spec. 1.—This principle, merely introduced in this style, is extended in the reporting style to some other curves, and forms a convenient way of writing many phrases ending with the words *there* and *their*. (See Chapter IX, 98.)

2. The trebled ‿ may also be used in the word  *anthropology*, and its derivatives.

51. The letter ‿ may be made three times its usual length, to imply the addition of *gr*, in the words

longer,   linger,   anger.

Spec. 1.—This character should be made fully three times the length of ‿, to distinguish it clearly from the double-length ‿, implying *ndr*.

2. This principle may be applied to a few other words, such as *finger, stronger, hunger*. (R. L. Ninth, 56.)

The full form must be used where a vowel follows the *gr*, as in the words ‿ *angry*, ‿ *hungry*.

WRITING EXERCISE NINTH.

After, rafter, laughter, alter, falter, filter, Easter. Elder, wilder, wilderness, under, render, tender, ponder, understanding. Enter, entertain, intersperse. Counter, encounter. Alexander. Matter, mutter, letter, latter, fetter, shatter, diameter, flutter, fritter, splendor.

Winter, wintry, enter, entry, sunder, sundry, meander, Lysander. Rend-er, render, defender. Lottery, literary. Fester, pester, master, luster, illiterate. Sister, disaster, boaster, jester, haunter, hunter, binder, bindery, founder, foundry. Neither, another, anger, linger, longer, finger. Angry, hunger, hungry, stronger. Anthropology, anthropological, misanthropy, anthropomorphic, anthropoid.

> *Ask mother erth why oaks wer made*
> *Taller and stronger than the weeds they shade.*

The 'excentric' man is generally the pioneer of mankind, cutting his way the first into gloomy depths of unexplored sience, overcoming difficulties that woud check meaner spirits, and then holding up the liht of his knolege to guide thousands who, but for him, woud be wandering about in all the uncertainty of ignorance, or be held in the fetters of some selfish policy which they had not of themselves the ability to thro off.

Everything in the universe, both of mind and matter, exists in reference to certain fixt principles, which are calld laws of order, originating in the great First Cause, and thence emanating thro'out all creation.

The grand degrees of all existences ar what is natural, human, Divine. The three grand divisions of all natural

CHAPTER V.

things ar erths, waters, and atmospheres. The three kingdoms of nature ar the mineral, the vegetable, and the animal. The three divisions of the animal kingdom are into those that creep and walk on the erth, those that swim, and those that fly. Each of these divisions is divided into trines, according to which all things exist and subsist.

ANECDOTE. — "How do you know," said a traveler to a poor, wandering Arab of the desert, "that there is a God?" "In the same manner," he replied, "that I trace the footsteps of an animal, — by the prints it leavs upon the sand."

> Ill fares the land, to hasening ills a prey,
> Where welth accumulates and men decay.
> Princes or lords may flurish or may fade:
> A breth can make them, and a breth has made;
> But a bold pesantry, their country's pride,
> When once destroyed, can never be supplied.

WRITING EXERCISE TENTH.

The favorit idea of a genius among us is of one who never studies, or who studies nobody can tel when, — at midniht, or at od times and intervals, — and now and then strikes out, at a heat, as the phrase is, som wonderful production. This is a character that has figured largely in the history of our literature, in the persons of our Fieldings, our Savages, and our Steeles, — loos fello's about town, or loungers in the country, who slept in alehouses, and wrote in bar-rooms, — who took up the pen as a magician's wand to supply their wants, and when the presure of necessity was releved, resorted again to their carousals.

Now the truth is, as I shal take the liberty to state it, that genius wil study: it is that in the mind which wil study. Study, says Cicero, is the voluntary and vigorus application of the mind to any subject. Such study, such intense mental action, and nothing else, is genius. What tho the miht of genius appears in one decisiv blo, struc in som moment of hi debate, or at the crisis of a nation's peril? That mihty energy, tho it may hav heavd in the brest of a Demosthenes, was once a feebl infant's tho't. A mother's eye watchd over its dawning; a father's care garded its erly groth. It soon trod with youthful steps the halls of learning, and found other fathers to wake and to watch for it, — even as it finds them here. It went on; but silence was upon its path; and the deep struglings of the inward soul markt its progres, and the cherishing powers of nature silently minister to it. The elements around breathed upon it, and 'tucht it to finer issues.' The golden ray of heven fel upon it, and ripend its expanding faculties. The slo revolutions of years sloly aded to its collected tresures and energies, til, in its hour of glory, it stood forth embodid in the form of living, commanding, irresistible eloquence. The world wonders at the manifestation, and says 'strange, strange, that it shud com thus unso't, unpremeditated, unprepared.' But the truth is ther is no more miracl in it than ther is in the towering of the eminent forest tree, or in the floing of the mihty and irresistible river, or in the welth and the waving of the boundles harvest. — ORVILLE DEWEY.

CHAPTER VI.

PREFIXES.

52. The preceding principles of contraction apply largely to all classes of words, and to all parts of words. In plain and simple Saxon speech, they will give great power to the writer. But we have a large class of words in the language that are longer, and composed of distinct parts,—a *root* or primitive form, with numerous derivatives, formed by the addition of prefixes or affixes. Thus, from the root *form* we have the derivatives *inform, deform, reform, misform, misinform, formed, forming, former, formal, formalist, formation, information, reformation,* &c., to the number of nearly a hundred in all. (R. L. Tenth, 58.)

53. Now it is not necessary to contract many of the particles used as prefixes and affixes, as many of them are sufficiently brief when written by the principles already given. Yet, some of them occur with greater frequency, and it has been found to be convenient to furnish them with briefer special signs.

a. They may be divided into two general classes. The first class is prefixed to the main body of the word, and are called prefixes or prefix signs. The second class forms endings of words, and are called affixes, or affix signs.

SIMPLE PREFIX SIGNS.

54. Prefix signs are either simple or compound. The simple prefixes are the following:—

con, com,	magni,	with,
contra,	magna,	intro,
in, im,	self,	trans.

CON AND COM.

55. The prefixes *con* and *com* are represented by the same signs.

Spec.—The use of the same sign for *con* and *com* cannot produce confusion, since these prefixes are mere variations of the same prefix, and never conflict in actual use. To illustrate,—we have the word *com*prise, but we cannot have the word *con*prise, because the letter *n* never precedes the letter *p*. So we have the word *con*tinue, but we cannot have such a word as *comtinue*, because the letter *m* cannot precede the letter *t*. So, in all cases where *con* occurs, *com* cannot be used, and *vice versa*.

56. We have two signs for these prefixes,— the first, a light stroke in the direction of \, and one-third the length of this letter; the second, a stroke of the same length in the direction of the /. They are joined in the outline, as will be seen in the following examples:—

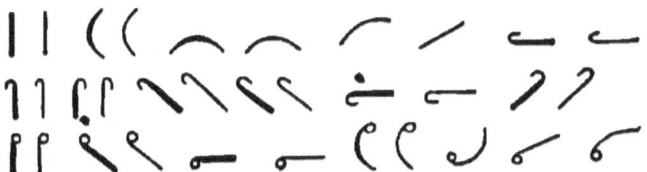

console, concede, consider, conduce, compress, comply.

Sec. 1. *a.*—The sign \ is used for *con* and *com* in the following words, and in many others given in Writing Exercise 11: *comprise, compress, comprehend, complain, conclude, conglomerate, construct.* (R. L. Tenth, 59.)

b. The sign \ is used for *con* and *com* in all words in which these prefixes are followed by

and some other characters.

c. Use \ also for *con* and *com* in the following words:—

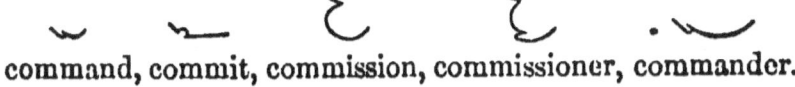

command, commit, commission, commissioner, commander.

2. The second form, ⁄, struck downward, is used for *con* and *com* in the following words: *connect, concur, concave, conduce, condense, continue, confess, converge, convex, conceive, consult* (R. L. Tenth, 60), and in all words in which these prefixes are followed by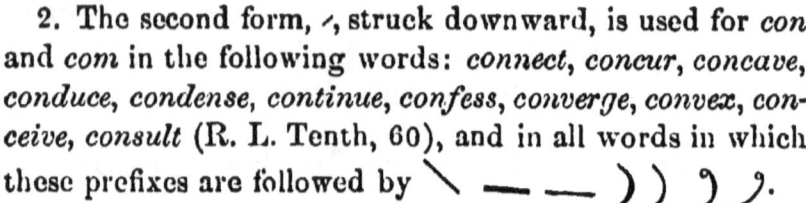

3. This sign is struck upward in the following words:—

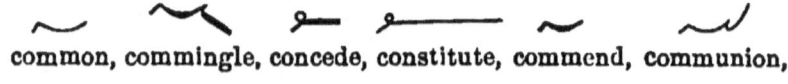
common, commingle, concede, constitute, commend, communion,

and in all words in which *con* or *com* are followed by ⌣ ⌣ ⌣ ⌒ ⌒ , such as *commonplace, communicate, commendable, constitute, commentator.*

4. The following words are exceptional: ⌢— *concomitant,* ⌢⌢ *uncommon,* ⌢⌢⌢ *intercommunicate.*

Rem. 1.—It should be observed —

a. That the sign is used for *con* and *com* in all cases in which it can conveniently be used, so that this form always takes the precedence when it can be employed.

b. That the second form, ⁄, is struck downward whenever it can be joined easily in this direction, and that the downward form is preferred to the upward.

c. That the upward form is used for convenience, and only in a few words.

Rem. 2. — The prefixes *con* and *com* are of greater use than all the other prefixes given in the table, since they are used in thousands of words, many of which are of frequent occurrence. They also occur connected with other prefixes, and form the basis of nearly all the compound prefixes which are treated of in the end of this chapter.

CON AND COM RADICAL.

57. In some words *con* and *com* form the root, or part of the root, of the word, as in the words *conical* from *cone*, and *comical* from the Latin *comicus*, allied to the Greek *komos*. Such words should be written in full.

Spec.—Words in which *con* and *com* are radical generally contain a single *n* or *m* followed by a vowel. The following are the principal words of this class. *Coma, comb, come, comet, comic, comity.* *Con* (to fix in the mind): *conch, cone, Congo, cony,* and their derivatives. (R. L. Tenth, 62.)

Rem.—Words in which *com* is followed by a root commencing in *m* in most cases drop the *m* of the root. Thus *com-ence, com-union, com-ute,* for *commence, communion, commute.* The word *comity* is written in full, while the word *committee* loses both *m*'s.

Rem. 2.—The word *connect* and its derivatives lose both *n*'s in the same manner, but *connive, connatural,* and other words in which *con* is followed by *n* in the root, retain the second *n*.

WRITING EXERCISE ELEVENTH.

In the following Words, use the sign \ for *Con* and *Com*.

Comprise, compress, comprehend, complain, conclude, conglomerate, construct (R. L. Tenth, 59), *contribute, contract, consecrate, consider, conspicuous, consecutive, consequential, consult, concert, consummate, consist. Combine, compose, conscious, conjure* (zhr), *contrive, control, console, concise, concision, concession, noncommital, commercial, conquest, conclave, concrete, congress, confront, converse, command, commanding, commander, commit, committee, commission, commissioner.*

In the following Words, use the /, written downwards.

Connecting, concurring, concord, concave, concavity, conducing, condensing, condign, condemn, contain, contaminate, continue, converge, converse', conversing, convince, convene, confine, confide, confound, confessing, confidant, convex, convict, conceive, conciliate, consult, consulting.

Use the / upward in the following Words.

Common, commonplace, common sense, community, communicate, commend, commendatory, commending, commendable, commingle, concede, conceding, constitute, constituted, constituent, constabulary.

Miscellaneous.

Concomitant, uncommon, commodore, comfort, conquer, conquerer, unconquered, unconquerable, commemorate, commensurate, comment, commodious, commodity, community, compact, comprehensive, commute, compute, comparative, comparatively, compatible, compatibly, compatriot, compound, compensate, competent, compliance, component, comport, compressible, compromise, compel, compulsive, comrade. Conceal, concentrative, concessive, conclave, conclusive, concord, concrete, concupiscence, concurrent, confessor, confirm, conform, conservative, considerable, consociate, consistent, consolatory.

Every evil that we conquer is a benefactor. The Sandwich Ilander believd that the strength and valor of the enemy he killd passd into himself. Spiritually it is so with us, for we gain strength from every temptation we succesfully resist. In matters of great concern, and which must be done, ther is no surer evidence of a weak mind than irresolution. To be always intending to liv a new life, and never to set about it, this is the folly of follies.

BUTY. — The hih and divine buty which can be lovd without effeminacy is that which is found in combination with a human will, and never separate. Buty is the mark God sets upon virtue. Every heroic act is also decent, and causes the place and the by-standers to shine. We ar taut by great action that the univers is the property of every individual in it. Every rational creature has all nature for his dowry and estate. It is his, if he wil. He may divest himself of it; he may creep into a corner, and abdicate his kingdom, as most men do, — but he is entitled to the world by his constitution. In proportion to his tho't and will, he takes up the world into himself.

"All those things for which men plow, bild, or sail obey virtue," said an ancient historian. "The winds and waves," said Gibbon, "ar always on the side of the ablest navigators." So are the sun and moon, and all the stars of heven.—EMERSON.

CONTRA.

58. The prefix *contra* is used only in a few words, and they follow the analogy of ⌒ *contradict*, ⌒ *contravene*.

SPEC.—The following words have the prefix ⌒: *contraband, contradict, contradistinguish, contrary, contravene, contraversion,* and their derivatives. (R. L. Tenth, 63.)

IN AND IM.

59. Of the two forms given in the table for the prefixes *in* and *im*, the former is used wherever convenient, as in

income, index, impulse.

The latter is used mainly before ⌒ ⌐ ⌐ ⌐ ⌐ ⌐ ⌐, as in

immortal, inbred, impress, imply, incline, impart.

SPEC. 1.—Use the ⟩ in *imbue, impugn, inexcusable, inexact, indomitable, ineffable, invest, inestimable, innocent, ineradicable, inartificial.* (R. L. Tenth, 64, *a*.)

CHAPTER VI.   109

2. Use the ⌒ in *imbrue, imprint, implead, ingress, increase, inclose, immense.* (R. L. Tenth, 64, *b*.)

REM. 1.—The prefixes *in* and *im* are mere variations of the same original *particle,* varied by the laws of euphony, as in the case of *con* and *com,* before noticed. Hence they can never conflict, only one form of the prefix being possible in any given case. The *im* almost always precedes *b, p,* and *m;* and *in* precedes other consonants. For this reason there is no need of distinguishing between *im* and *in* in writing words containing these prefixes.

REM. 2.—There are a few cases in which the prefix *in* precedes *b,* as in *inbred, inborn, inbreathe;* but these words do not take the prefix *im*: we have no such words as *imbreathe* or *imborn.*

60. Neither ⌒ nor ⌒ can be used before (, (, ⌒, ⌒, ⌒, ⌒, ⌒, ⌒, ⌒, ⌒. When either of these letters follows the prefixes *in* or *im,* a change of construction is necessary.

a. The use of the compounds ⌒, ⌒, ⌒ is avoided, the full forms ⌒ ⌒ ⌒ being used in their stead.

b. The compounds ⟩, ⟩, ⟩ are used wherever convenient, in place of the simple letters, as in

⟩ ⟩ ⟩

injure, insure, initial.

c. Before ⟋ and ⟋, the prefix is written in full, and also before (, (, ⌒, ⌒ when the compound forms ⟩ ⟩ cannot be used.

SPEC. 1.—Under the principle mentioned in section 60,

a, we have such words as *iniquity, inquiry, indelible, intolerant*, and many others. (R. L. Tenth, 65, *a*.)

2. Under section 60, *b*, we have only a few words: *injure, injured, injury, insure, insured, insurance*, and *initial*. (R. L. Tenth, 65, *b*.) Under *c* we have such words as *inherent, inherit, inhabit, inweave, ingenuous, injudicious, inject, initiate, insatiable*. (R. L. Tenth, 65, *c*.)

Rem.—Some of the words mentioned above are farther contracted in the reporting style.

61. *a*. When the prefix *in* or *im* precedes ⌠, \, ⌐ or ⌐, the circle may be written on the R-hook side, as in

inspire, insect, institute.

Spec. 1.—This principle applies to the words *insupportable, inspect, insecure, instead, install, instate*. Compare, however, with these the words *instruct, instrument*. (R. L. Tenth, 66, *a*.)

2. The same principle may be also applied to the signs ⌠, \, and ⌐ in such words as *insubordinate, insignia, incidental*, and some others. (R. L. Tenth, 66, *b*.)

b. The circle is also written in the prefix ⌒ and ⌐ when followed by the curves),), ⌒, ⌒, (, ⌣, ╱, and the ╱, as in the words *inseverity, insufferable, insist, insincerity, insult, insurmountable*. (R. L. Tenth, 66, *c*.)

62. *a*. In some words commencing with *im*, these letters are radical and should not be writ-

CHAPTER VI.   111

ten with the prefix. Such words are *image, imitate*, and their derivatives.

b. The prefix *in*, on the contrary, is followed by a vowel, and the prefix sign may, if necessary, be attached to the vowel that commences the *root*.

SPEC. 1.—Where the prefix *in* is followed by a vowel, the vowel may be omitted before most of the consonants, as in the words *inaccurate, inanimate, inarticulate, inelegant, inexpedient, inordinate*. (R. L., sec. 68, *a*.)

2. But where the *in* precedes the *b, p*, or *m*, with an intervening vowel, the vowel should be written, to enable the reader to distinguish at a glance between *in* and *im*, — for he expects *im* to precede |, |, and ⌒, and would read ⋃ , *impel* sooner than *i*nappli—.

This principle applies to such words as *inapplicable, inapposite, inebriate, inoperative, inopportune, inimical, inimitable*. (R. L., sec. 68, *b*.)

63. *a.* When the prefix *im* is followed by *m*, as in *immaterial*, the *m* of the *root* is always retained.

b. The same principle applies to the prefix *in*. When followed by *n* in the *root*, the second *n* is written.

Ex.—*Immature, immeasurable, immediate, immense, immigrate, innocent, innocuous, innovate, innumerable.* (R. L., 69.)

INTRA, INTRI, INTRO, ETC.

64. The hook of the ⌒ is dropped after *in* in the prefix *intro;* and the use of this mode of contraction is extended to many words commencing with *intra, intrans, intre,* and *intri,* as in the following

Examples.

intransitive, introduce, intrigue, intrepid, intrude.

SPEC.—The principal words that are so contracted in the Note-Taker's style are *intractable, intrench, intricate, intrinsic, intromit, introspective, introvert, intrust,* with the examples given above, and the words derived from them. (R. L., sec. 70.)

MAGNI AND MAGNA.

65. These prefix signs apply to only a few words. *Magni* is written upward, *magna,* downward, as in  *magnificent,* *magnanimous.*

SPEC.—The remaining words commencing with this prefix are *magnanimity, magna-charta, magnify, magnific, magnitude,* with their immediate derivatives. (R. L., 71.)

CHAPTER VI.

SELF, WITH, AND TRANS.

66. *a.* The prefix) (*self*) may be written either upward or downward, as in ⟨ *selfish*, ⟨‿ *self-admiring*. The direction in which this prefix is written is determined by the same principles that apply to the use of the upward and downward forms of) in other cases. (See Elements of Tachyg., Chap. X.)

SPEC. — This prefix occurs in the words *self-abhorrence, self-conceit, self-denial, self-esteem, self-evident, self interest, selfish, self-love, self-possession, self-same, self-will,* and a few others. (R. L., sec. 72.)

b. The prefix ⟨ (*with*) admits of no variation, but is used as in the word ⌒ *withdraw,*

c. Trans (⟜). The circle in which this prefix ends may be written on either side of the stem, following the rules that determine the proper use of the circle in other cases.

transgress, transact, translucent.

SPEC. 1.—*Intrans* loses the hook as shown above in section 64.

2. When the *trans* is followed by a *root* commencing in *s*, as in *transcend*, only one *s* is written. The *trans* in this

case loses its *s* in pronunciation, and sometimes in our common orthography, as when we write *tran*-scribe for *trans*-scribe, but these words are written as though pronounced *trans-end, trans-cribe.*

3. Other words containing this prefix are *transform, transfer, transfuse, tranship, transition, translate, transmigrate, transplant, transport, transverse,* and a few others with derivatives. (R. L., sec. 73.)

Excep. 1.— *Trancient* and its derivatives drop the *s*, as it is dropped in speech.

2. *Transit* is written ⌒ↄ—.

WRITING EXERCISE TWELFTH.

Contra.—*Contradict, contradictions, contradicting, contradistinguish, contravene.*

Im.—*Imbecile, imbitter, imbosom, imbrue, imbue, immaculate, immature, immeasurable, immediate, immemorial, immense, immigrant, imminent, immoderate, immodest, immoral, immortal, immovable, immutable, impair, impartial, impart, impassable, impeach, impel, imperceptible, imperfect, impertinent, imperative, impious, implacable, implant, implead, implicit, implore, imply, import, importance, important, impost, impressible, imprudent, impugn, impunity.*

In.—*Inaccessible, inaccurate, inactive, inadequate, inadmissible, inalienable, inalterable, inapplicable, inappropriate, inarticulate, inaudible, inaugural, inauspicious, inborn, inbreathe, inbred, incapable, incapacitate, incisive, incline, inclose, income, incorporeal, incorrect, incrust, incredible, increase, incredulous, incredulity, inculpate, incurable, indebted, indecent, indefatigable, indelible, indefensible, indelicate, indestructible, indicate, indictable, indiscriminate, indisposed, indissoluble, indolent, induce, indwell, inebriate, ineffable, inequality, inert, inertness, inestimable, inevitable, inexcusable, inexpedient, inexpressible, inextinguishable, inextricable, infallible, infamous, infatuate, infect, infer, inferior, inflame, infest, inflict, influence, inform, infract, ingrate, inimitable, iniquity, initial, innocence, innovate, innumerable, inofficious, inoperative, inordinate, inquire, inroad, insatiable, inscribe, inscrutable, inseparable, insolvency, inspire, insult, insure, insurmountable, intellect, intemperate, intend, intimate, intimidate, intuitive, invalid, invariable, inventive, investigate, invent, invincible, involuntary, invulnerable.*

Incendiary, incense, instruct, inspect, insect, inspire, inspirit, institute, insubordinate, instantaneous, incentive.

NOTE.—The prefix is not used in the words *incessant* and *incest.*

Magna-l, Self, With, Intra-l-o, Trans.

Magnify, magnificent, magnificence, magnitude, magnanimous, magnanimity.

Self-denial, self-denying, selfish, self-admiring, self-conceit, celf-conscious, self-esteem, self-evident, self-interest, selfishness, self-same, self-will.

Withdraw, withstand, withhold, within, without. Herewith, therewith, wherewithal.

Introduce, intromit, introcession, intrinsic, intrinsically, intrench, intrepid, intricacy, intrigue, introvert, intrude, intrusive, intransitive, intransmissible, intransmutable.

Transact, transatlantic, transcend, transcendent, transcendentalism, transcribe, transcript, transept, transfer, transform, transfuse, transgress, transitive, translate, translucent, transmigration, transmissible, transmit, transmute, transparent, transplant, transport, transpose, transverse.

OBEY ORDERS.—*A brave veteran officer, reconnoitering a battery which was considered impregnable, and which it was necessary to storm, laconically answered the engineers, who were endeavoring to dissuade him from the attempt, "Gentlemen, you may think and say what you please; all I know is that the American flag must be hoisted on the ramparts tomorrow morning, for I have the order in my pocket."*

COMPOUND PREFIXES.

67. Compound prefixes consist of the simple prefixes already given and a preceding particle. Most of them are compounds of *com* or *con*, with a preceding *de, dis, in, mis,* or *un.* The most important forms are given in the following table:—

COMPOUND PREFIX SIGNS.

decom,
discom,
discon,
incom,
incon,

miscon,
recon,
irrecon,
recog,

rein,
uncon,
uncom,
circum.

68. The use of those compound prefixes which end in *com* or *con* is analogous to that of the simple forms in similar cases. The following cases, however, deserve notice.

a. The stroke for *con* or *com* in the compound prefixes may assume any of the variations assumed by the simple prefixes so far as convenient.

SPEC.—Such variations occur in the words *discontinue, inconstant, inconsistant, uncontaminated.* (R. L., sec. 74.)

b. The ╱ in the prefix *recom* may be struck downward in the words ⌒ *recommend*, ⌒ *recommence*, and their derivatives.

69. *a. Circum* (treated as though spelled *circom*) is contracted in some words by omitting the *cum*, as in ⌒ *circumstance.*

b. As *circum* is classed with the *con* and *com* prefixes, so also may *incum* and *recum* be written as though spelled *incom* and *recom*, as in the words *incumbent, recumbent, encumber.* (R. L., sec. 75.)

c. Recog is used only in the word *recognize* and its derivatives.

70. There are other modifications and combinations not given in the table arising out of the union of prefix signs that will be easily understood.

Spec. 1.—*Rein* and *reim* admit of a freedom in the use of the ⊃ the same as explained in case of the simple prefixes.

Ex.—*Reimburse, reimprint, reinforce, reinhabit, reinsert, reinsure, reinstall.* (R. L., sec. 76.)

2.—*Accom* may be written with or without the *com*, as in

accomplish, accompany, accommodate.

CHAPTER VI.

3. Other compounds that occur in a few words are *un-contra* in *uncontradicted*, *unself* in *unselfish*, *unmagni* in *unmagnified*, *untrans* in *untranslated;* *misin*, *mistrans* in ⌒— *misinformed,* ⌒⊃— *mistranslated;* *unaccom* in *unaccommodated, unaccompanied.* (R. L., sec. 77.)

WRITING EXERCISE THIRTEENTH.

Decompose, discompose, discontinue, inconstancy, misconceive, misconstrue, reconcile, reconstruct, irreconcilable, recognize, reinvest, unconscious, unconcerned, circumference, circumstances, circumcise, circumnavigate. Incongruous, incomplete, incumbent, incombustible, incompatible, recommence, recommend, unconstrained, unconstitutional, disconnected, uncontroverted, uncontradicted. Accompanied, unaccompanied, accomplished, unaccomplished, selfishly, unselfishly, unmagnified, misinformed, misinterpreted, misconstrued, uncircumcised, unrecognized.

Reinvest, reimburse, reimprint, reinfect, reinhabit, reinsert, reinsure, reinvigorate. Encumber, incumbent, recumbent, inconstant, inconsistent, uncontaminated.

MODERN REPUBLICS.—*Where ar the republics of modern times, which clustered round immortal Italy? Venice and Genoa exist but in name. We stand the latest, and, if we fail, probably the last experiment of self-government by the peeple. We have begun it under circumstances of the most auspicius nature. We ar in the vigor of youth. Our constitutions hav never bin enfeebled by the vices or luxuries of the old world. Such as we ar, we hav bin from the beginning,—simple, hardy, intelligent, accustomd to self-government, and self-respect. The Atlantic rolls between us and any formidable foe. Within our own territory, stretching throo many degrees of latitude and longitude, we hav the choice of many products, and many means of independence. Alredy has the age caut the spirit of our institutions. It has infused itself into the life-blood of Europe, and warmed the sunny plains of France and the lolands of Holland. It has tucht the philosophy of Germany, and the North, and, moving onward to the South, has opened to Greece the lessons of her better days. Can it be that America under such circumstances can betray herself? that she is to be aded to the catalog of republics the inscription upon whose ruins is 'They were, but they are not.' Forbid it, my countrymen: forbid it Heven!* — STORY.

WRITING EXERCISE FOURTEENTH.

EFFECTS OF SUCCESS.—*If you wud revenge yourself on those hoo hav slihted you, be successful. It is a bitter satire on their want of judgment to sho that you can do without them. This is a wound to the self-love of proud, inflated peeple; and you must reckon on their hatred, as they wil never forgiv you.*

RAISING RENT. — *"Sir, I intend to raise your rent,"* sed a land-holder to one of his tenants, to which he replied, — *"I am very much obliged to you, for I cannot raise it myself."*

PRINCIPAL AND INTEREST.—*A detor, when askt to pay his creditor, observd to him that it was not his interest to pay the principal, nor his principle to pay the interest.*

VARIETIES. — *To promote an unworthy person disgraces humanity. The human mind is a mirror of the incomprehensible Deity. The reason that many persons want their desires is because their desires want reason. Happy ar the miseries that end in joy, and blessed ar the joys that hav no end.*

BOUNDARIES OF KNOLEGE.—*Human reason very prop-*

_erly refuses to giv its assent to any thing without evidence of its truth. Yet the powers of reason ar limited on all subjects of inquiry. The astronomer finds a difficulty in getting from the solar system to a clear idea of the outlying univers; the chemist in proceeding from matter to its mysterious essence; and the physiologist in advancing from the body to the soul. These three kingdoms of knolege border on other kingdoms unknown to natural sience. Our minds ar so constituted that, after having traverst the material creation, and perceivd, sientifically, the very boundaries of matter, where it is adjoined to spirit, it can elevate itself by power constantly given by God to the lower boundaries of spirit life, and from thence ascend, step by step, to a knolege of the great I Am, whom to kno ariht, and to love supremely, is the hihest good of man.

CHAPTER VII.

AFFIXES.

71. The class of words introduced in the last chapter, which consist of a *root*-word varied by means of prefixes, are farther modified by annexing particles, called affixes or suffixes.

The terminations *ing, ed, ous, ment* in the words *knowing, wretched, righteous, fragment* are familiar examples.

It is not necessary to provide special signs for all of these terminations, as most of them are sufficiently brief when written in accordance with the general principles of the art. Yet, contracted modes of writing some of them have been adopted, and are found to be very useful.

72. The following table contains the most important of these signs. Like the prefixes, they may be either simple or compound.

TABLE OF AFFIX SIGNS.

SIMPLE.		COMPOUND.	
⌒	ment,	♪	mental,
⸦	cient,	⌣	ular,
♃	self,	⌣	ularly,
⸜	soever,	⸝	nation,
⌒	with,	⸝	ulation,
⌒	ward,	∪	tional,
⌣	ure,	⌣⌒	tionality,
⌣	ural, ual,	⸝	fication.
⌣	uraly, ually,		

MENT, MENTAL, MENTARY.

73. *a.* The affix *ment* is a half-length ⌒. In forming *mental*, a small hook is added, which may be considered a relic of the *n* hook more freely used in the reporting style. These signs may be written either upward or downward, as ⌒ is written in other cases, following the laws

already given to govern the direction of this letter. (See Elements, p. 91.)

Ex.—*Detriment, detrimental, ornament, ornamental, sentiment, sentimental, monument, embarrassment, sacrament, raiment.* (R. L., sec. 79.)

b. We have also the terminations *mentary* and *mentality,* as in *elementary, mentality,* written ⌞, &c.

c. The plural is formed by adding the circle, as ⌞ *elements.*

CIENT, TIENT, ETC.

74. *a.* This affix, spelled in several ways, is written with the halved (and *n* hook. We have, also, *ciently* written in analogy with *men-. tal.* These terminations are of frequent occurrence.

Ex.—*Ancient, anciently, trancient, patient, proficient, sufficient, sufficiently.* (R. L., sec. 80.)

b. In a similar manner are formed the terminations ⌐ *dent* and ⌐ *dental,* ⌐ *gent* and *gently* ⌐, and others, as in ⌐ *accident,* ⌐ *accidental,* ⌐ *urgent,* ⌐ *urgently.*

c. This form of contraction may also be applied in such words as *constant, constantly, instant, instantly, intent, intently.* (R. L., sec. 81.)

Rem.—The forms (and (‿/, and others of this class, are regularly formed, in accordance with principles developed in the reporting style. While the (is halved to imply *t*, a hook is added to represent the *n*, which is read before the implied *t*. This method of contraction is too much involved to be used indiscriminately in this style, but it may be applied safely in the case of a few terminations, as explained in this section.

SOEVER.

75. The use of this affix is uniform, and will be easily understood from the following examples:—

whensoever, howsoever, wheresoever, whosoever, whosesoever.

SELF AND WITH.

76. The signs for these affixes are the same as the signs for the corresponding prefixes, given in Chapter VI.

Self may be written in either direction, as in ⟋ *himself,* ⟋⟋ *his own self.* The plural is formed by adding the circle, as ⟋⟋ *ourselves.*

Ex.—*Herewith, wherewithal, themselves, herself, whatsoever.* (R. L., sec. 82.)

WARD.

77. The sign for this affix is formed by making the latter part of the stem of ╱ heavy, thus ╱.

Ex.— ╱ *onward,* ╱ *forward.* The word *toward* is written irregularly, thus ⌒.

URE.

78. This affix is of very frequent use, and applies to nearly all words ending in the sounds *yr*, whether written *ure, ier, ior, iar,* or *eur,* as

nature, pannier, culture, cultured,

grandeur, familiar, peculiar, pictures.

URAL, URALLY, UAL, AND UALLY.

79. These affixes belong to only a very few words, and no confusion can result from the use

of the same form for *ural* and *ual*. The form of this affix is a large hooked ⌒, implying the ⌒, in analogy with the large hook on the ⌒. The forms *urally* and *ually* add the tick, in analogy with the words *any* and *many*.

Examples.

natural, naturally, gradual, gradually.

80. *a.* The affix sign for *ular* is double length, and the adverbial form adds an ⌒, thus: regular, regularly.

b. Some words ending in *ular* do not have the sound of ⌒, and are written without this affix. Such words are *angular, circular.*

Miscel. Ex. — *Mutual, spiritual, scriptural, secular, vernacular, angular, circular.* (R. L., sec. 83.)

UATION AND ULATION.

81. *a.* These are written with large final hooks, the former on a single-length, the latter on a double-length, letter.

Ex.— graduation, congratulation.

b. The use of these forms is much more frequent than those given in section 80, and their use is limited only in such words as *osculation*, where the sound of ⌣ is not distinctly heard.

Ex.—*Situation, emulation, modulation, stipulation, attenuation, extenuation.* (R. L., sec. 84.)

TIONAL AND TIONALLY.

82. *a.* The terminations *tional* and *tionally* are contracted into *shl*, written ⌣ as given in the table of affixes, or with ⌒, as in

national, nationality, professional, professionally.

b. In words where the *s* in *sional* has the sound of *zh*, the heavy signs ⌣ and ⌒ are used, as in ⌣ *occasional,* ⌒ *provisional.*

FICATION.

83. This termination is written *fshn*. The large hook is used for *shn*, as in the terminations *uation* and *ulation*, given above, thus ⌒ *sanctification*.

Ex.—*Sensational, traditional, rational, notional, justification, rectification.*   (R. L., sec. 85.)

THE SHN HOOK.

84. *a.* A large final hook may be used for the termination *shn* (spelled *tion, sion, tian, cian,* &c.) on most of the consonants.

b. This hook is written on the right side of | | \\, on the upper side of —, —, and /, and on the inside of the curves.

Examples.

objection, option, section, addition, confession,

revision, proposition, omission, recognition, coalition.

Spec. 1.— The *shn* hook is used—

a. Where no vowel precedes the termination, as in the words ⌒ *tension,* ⌒ *mention,* ⌒ *deception,* and other words given above.

b. Where the *shn* is preceded by the vowels ă, ĕ, or ĭ (◡. or ⌒), as in the words ⌊ *passion,* ⌒ *discretion,* ⌒ *rendition,* ⌒ *mission.*

Ad. Ex. — *Extortion, emersion, contortion, conception, connection, discretionary, missionary, visionary, dictionary.* (R. L., sec. 86.)

2. Some words, in which the letters \ or | precede the termination *shn*, drop the \ or | before taking the hook, as ⌒ *sanction,* ⌒ *instruction,* ⌒ *redemption.*

a. The \ is dropped in a few words only in this style, and in these it is preceded by — or ⌣. They are *instruction, destruction, destructive, sanction.* (R. L., sec. 87.)

b. The | is dropped after ⌒ in all such words as *consumption, assumption, presumption, redemption.* (R. L., sec. 88.)

REM. — It will be observed that the *p* in words in which it is dropped forms no radical part of the word, but is inserted in our common orthography because the sound is necessary to the easy pronunciation of the word, — that is, when the sound (follows ⌒, without an intervening vowel, the sound of *p* is inserted mechanically in passing from the ⌒ to the (. But this sound is not needed in the writing, because it will be easily inferred.

85. A large class of words end in the terminations *ation, otion,* and *ution.* These are contracted in the reporting style by writing the ⌐, \, ¯, and ⌃ for *ation, otion, and ution,* omitting the ⌒, as in the words

negation, approbation, dissipation, emanation, emotion, allusion.

SPEC. 1. — This mode of contraction is not entirely in harmony with the principles of this style, and should be used sparingly, if at all. Especially should short words, such as *nation, notion, motion* be written in full.

2. There are some other words which end in *shn* which should be written in full: these are —

a. Those in which the termination *shn* is not an affix, but part of the original word, as in

ocean,   Prussian,   Grecian.

b. Some words ending in *cession*, as *cession* and *session*, *secession*.

REM. 1.—The method of writing the affixes given in this chapter enables the writer to distinguish between many words which would be written with the same outlines if all words ending in *shn* were written with the same mode of contraction, as is the case in phonography. This mode* of writing gives, for instance, the same form to the words *motion, mission, emotion* and *emission, dissipation* and *deception, dissolution* and *desolation, elision, illusion, elation, lotion,* and *allusion,* and many others, except as some more or less arbitrary distinctions are employed.

REM. 2.— It is not easy to determine to how great an extent the termination *shn* may be omitted with advantage in this style. It may be of use to certain persons, in case of words of frequent occurrence, to omit it, while for other persons it may be unsafe. This termination is added so easily that, in most kinds of writing, the speed of writing gained by its omission in the cases mentioned would be very small indeed.

---

* *The Phonographic.*

CHAPTER VII. 133

WRITING EXERCISE FIFTEENTH.

Fragment, figment, impediment, raiment, ornament, movement, achievement, reinstatement, ailment, ointment, basement, abasement, casement, element, filament, detriment, sentiment, sacrament, monument, nutriment, instrument.

Detrimental, sacramental, instrumental, fundamental, ornamental, elemental, alimentary, elementary, instrumentality.

Ancient, patient, transient, proficient, deficient, efficient, sufficient, anciently, patiently, transiently, quotient.

Accident, accidental, regent, urgent, urgently, gentle, gently, extent, instant, instantly, resident, residents, instants.

Himself, herself, itself, ourself, ourselves, yourselves.

Whosoever, whensoever, wheresoever, howsoever, whosesoever, whatsoever. Wherewith, herewith, therewith. Inward, outward, rearward, forward, backward, onward, heavenward. Rewarder, inwardly, outwardly, rewarding, forwarding.

Figure, nature, stature, torture, verdure, moisture, vesture, pasture, posture, mixture, fixture. Natures, mixtures. Figured, natured. Natural, structural, scriptural. Naturally.

Familiar, familiarly, familiarity. Pannier, soldier, soldierly, grandeur.

Adventures, adventurous, culture, cultured, sculptured, peculiar, peculiarly.

Gradual, gradually, effectual, effectually, spiritual, spiritually, annual, annually, habitual, eventual.

Oracular, vernacular, particular, ocular, ocularly, jocu-

lar, jocularly, titular, globular, regular, irregular, unpopular, secular, secularly, secularize. Graduation, congratulation, tribulation, speculation, regulation, modulation, population, stipulation, accentuation, fluctuation, stimulation, emulation, situation, evacuation, attenuation, extenuation, perpetuation, expostulation, matriculation.

Notional, rational, sensational, traditional, emotional, professional, provisional, professionally, provisionally, occasional, occasionally, nationality, sensuality.

Mortification, justification, sanctification, edification, fructification, rectification, ratification.

A BURLESQUE EDITORIAL. — *We have found thus early in our editorial life that the founding of a new periodical, and the preparation of the second number for the press, is quite a C-rious undertaking.*

Countless have been the caucuses, conventions, councils, confederations, convocations, collections, conversations, concertings, cogitations, conferences, contrivings, combinations, and concatinations, considered called for in composing, concocting, collecting, compiling, combining, concentrating, condensing, and copying the copious contents of our columns; cautiously clearing from chaff, clarifying from coarseness, and carving from clumsiness, the contributions and communications; considering ourselves caterers to a capricious crowd, comprising censorious, cynical, crabbed, crusty, captious, cringing, canting, carping, cavilling, contemptible critics; courteous, candid, careful, considerate, compassionate contemporaries; cheerful, civil correspondents, and cool, calculating, competent contributors. Completely comprehending our consequence, confident of the countenance and commendation of the charitable as a *c*ompensation for our *c*omplicated *c*ares, we have *c*arefully *c*ompiled a *c*ongruous *c*ollection of *c*hoice *c*ontributions, *c*oncise, *c*reditable *c*ommunications and *c*apital *c*onundrums and *c*harades, *c*alculated to *c*onvince *c*ritics, *c*avillers, and *c*otemporaries of our *c*are for their *c*omfort, and *c*onsideration for their *c*onvenience. *C*ondemning *c*ontroversy, *c*alumny, *c*ontention, and *c*umbrous or *c*areless *c*ommunications, we have *c*onfidently *c*ast ourselves upon the *c*onsideration of the *c*rowd.

WRITING EXERCISE SIXTEENTH.

Confession, profession, passion, vision, division, revision. Position, opposition, imposition, proposition, disposition. Precision, decision, excision, circumcision.

Mission, omission, commission, remission, redemption, exemption, preemption, distention, extention, ascension, mention, tension, dissension, pension. Recognition, amunition, coalition, comprehension. Ambition, prohibition, option, adoption, deception, passion, inception, reception, action, auction, section, attraction, fraction, friction, affection, inflection, infliction, affliction, retraction, dissection. Addition, edition, condition, perdition, tradition, superstition.

Instruction (omit the \ in this and the following words), *destruction, construction, rejection, dejection, conjunction, sanction, destruction.*

Contortion, extortion, cohesion, adhesion, derision, collision, collusion. Missionary, commissioner, dictionary, auctioneer, electioneer, elocutionist, abolitionism, abolitionist. Grecian, Prussian, Russian, Titian, ocean. Cession, secession, intercession, precession, misprision, elysian.

Argumentation, ornamentation. Passionate, fashionable, unfassioned, unimpassioned.

EDUCATION.—*Education means the development, perfection, and proper use of the body and mind. It relates to the training and guardianship of youth from infancy to mature age; to the influencing of the character, not only of individuals but of nations. The highest powers and noblest sentiments of our nature might remain forever dormant were they not developed and matured by the instruction and example of the wise and good. In a still wider sense, education may mean the whole training of the thoughts and affections by inward reflection and outward events and actions, by intercourse with men, 'by the spirits of the just made perfect,' by instruction from the word of God, and the training of the whole man for life and immortality.*—ANON.

ANALOGY.—*As in the succession of the seasons each, by the invariable laws of nature, affects the productions of what is next to come, so, in human life, every period of our age influences the happiness of that which is to follow. Virtuous youth generally brings forward accomplished and flourishing manhood, and such manhood passes off without uneasiness into respectable and tranquil old age. When nature is turned out of its regular course, disorder takes place in the moral world just as in the world of outward life. If the spring put forth no blossoms, in summer there will be no beauty, and in the autumn no fruit. If youth be trifled away without improvement, manhood will be contemptible, and old age miserable. If the beginnings of life have been vanity, its latter end can be no other than vexation of spirit.*—ANON.

CHAPTER VIII.

MISCELLANEOUS CONTRACTIONS.

86. In analogy with the affix *ward*, the stem of the ⌒ and ⌒ may be thickened near the end to imply *rd*, as in the words

word, heard, harden.

SPEC. — This principle applies to only a few words; and only in cases analogous to those given.

Ex.—Warden, hard, harder, unheard. (R. L., sec. 91.)

87. *a.* The letter *r* unites more or less closely with all pure consonants in such words as *ark, arm, orb, earn, furl.* This union of *r* with a following consonant is indicated by special signs, where followed by *d, t, s,* or *z,* by means of half-length characters, and the circle.

Two other cases of such union are followed with brief signs, as follows: —

b. Where *l* follows *r* without an intervening vowel, as in *curl, furl,* the *rl* may be written by making the upward ⁄ heavy, thus ⁄.

Spec.—The heavy *Ra* is used in such words as *moral, furl, relish, religious.* (R. L., sec. 92.)

c. When *n* unites with a preceding *r*, as in *earn*, it may be written by means of a final hook on either side of the ╱ or ╱, as in ⌐ *burn*, ⌐ *turn*.

Spec. 1.—There are many words in which this form of contraction may be used, and among them the following: *spurn, stern, adjourn, mourn, sworn.* (R. L., sec. 93.)

2. This hook cannot be used when the *n* is followed by a vowel, as in the word *journey*.

3. The *n* hook may be used on the ⟩ ⌐ ⌐ and ⌐ in writing the words ⟩ *then,* ⌐ *than,* ⌐ *men,* and ⌐ *one*.

Rem.—The use of the *n* hook is extended in the reporting style to other letters, and to cases where a vowel occurs before the *n*.

88. The final syllables *ance, ence, ans,* and *ens* are represented in some cases by writing the circle on the left or under side of a straight sign, as in

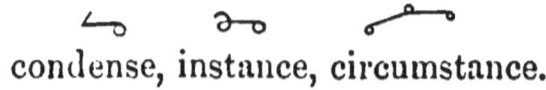

condense, instance, circumstance.

Spec. 1.—This form of contraction may be applied as in the words *expense, eloquence, interference, confidence,* and many other words. (R. L., sec. 94.)

2. This form of contraction is more useful after the up-

strokes /, /, /, and /, and the horizontals —, —, ⌒, and ⌒, than after the |, |, \, \, for the ⌒ joins so easily with the latter group of signs that less is gained by the contraction; yet it is used on | in such words as *expense*, where it is more convenient to write the second circle on the left, because the first circle occurs on the right side of the | . For a similar reason, it will be found convenient at times on |, \, \; but nothing will be gained by endeavoring to press this termination into use in all possible cases. Such words as *encumbrance, remembrance,* are best written

3. After a half-length character, this termination must be written in full, as in *acceptance.*

4. The word *once* is written, in analogy with the termination *ance.*

REM. 1.—The words *existence* and *consistence* drop the *n* without any direct reference to the principle stated in the preceding section, but merely because it cannot be easily joined in these cases.

89. *a.* A large final hook is used on the left and under side of the straight signs in the reporting style to express the sounds of *f* or *v*, generally in connection with the vocals ⌒ and ⌒. This form of contraction is employed in the Note-Taker's style to provide briefer outlines for the words *differ* and its derivatives,—*difference, different, indifferent,* &c. (R. L., sec. 95.)

b. This hook may also be employed in writing the words *give, forgive,* and their derivatives *given, forgiven, giving,* and *forgiving;* and in the words ⌡ *objective* and ⌠ *subjective;* but the ⌡ is used for the termination *ively* in *objectively, subjectively,* and elsewhere. (R. L., secs. 96, 106.)

DERIVATIVE WORD-SIGNS.

90. Derivatives formed from the words which are represented by word-signs, as given on page 82, follow the principles already given for writing affixes so far as they can be applied. The following specifications will sufficiently illustrate their use.

Spec. 1.—The plural of nouns and third singular of verbs is formed by adding the circle to the word-sign.

Ex.—*Objects, principles, improves, values, forms, things, generals.* (R. L., sec. 97.)

2. The termination *able,* as in other cases, is written either ⌠ or ⌣, as in *objectionable, improvable, remarkable, pleasurable, questionable.* (R. L., 98.)

3. The *ly* is added by ⌡, written either upward or downward, as *generally, gentlemanly, advantageously, largely, wholly.* (R. L., sec. 99.)

4. *a.* The words *form* and *question* shorten the final letter in adding the *ed;* but the — is added in the words *objected, subjected, improved, valued, acknowledged,* and *represented.* (R. L., sec. 100.)

b. The termination *ed* is omitted in writing the words *numbered, remarked,* and *advantaged.*

5. The termination *ing* is written as in other cases, by adding ◡ to the word-signs, as in *numbering, objecting, improving, enlarging.* (R. L., sec. 101.)

a. The terminations *less, ic,* &c. are formed regularly, as in *numberless, phonographic, tachygraphic, whilst, whence, generalissimo.* (R. L., sec. 102.)

7. *a.* The prefixes used in forming other derivatives from the word-signs given in the table need no special explanation. Their use will be understood from the following examples, as given in Reading Lesson Thirteenth, section 103: *unobjectionable, unprincipled, unvalued, unnumbered, unrepresented, disadvantage, anything, nothing.*

b. From the vocal word-signs we have the following: *altogether, although, also, always, whom, whose, whoever.* (R. L., sec. 104.)

CONTRACTED WORDS.

91. A few words not given in the table of word-signs are abbreviated by omitting a portion of the outline independently of the general rules of contraction. Those most employed in the Note-Taker's style are the following:—

already, almighty,   difficult, signify, significant,

practice, practicable, respect, outrage, useful, with their derivatives.

Spec. 1.— The principal derivatives formed from the contracted words given in this section are *difficulty, significance, insignificant, impracticable, respectful, respectively, outrageous, usefully.* (R. L., sec. 107.)

2. To these contracts may be added *eternal, internal, external,* and *fraternal,* which omit the ∕, and *children,* which omits the ∕. (R. L., sec. 108.)

COMPOUND WORDS.

92. Compound words are written in analogy with their primatives, and, so far as possible, joined into one outline. In cases where the compound is too long to be joined into one outline, the parts may be connected by an ordinary hyphen.

Spec.— Compound words are so numerous, and of such a varied character, that they cannot be treated of exhaustively here; yet, as they follow in all respects the same principles as simple words, they do not need special attention. The following examples furnish illustrations of the manner in which they are written: *self-knowledge, brute-mindedness, ever-deepening, forever-enduring, never-resting, fellow-workmen, body-guard, life-essence, life-purpose, God-given.* (R. L., sec. 109.)

CHAPTER VIII.

WRITING EXERCISE SEVENTEENTH.

Warding, rewarding, harden, harder, heard, unheard.

Marl, carl, girl, furl, moral, relish, religious, religions. Morn, corn, born, scorn, burn, turn, worn, mourn, bourne, return, adjourn, unlearn, sworn, concern, then, than, one, once, condense, eloquence, circumstance, interference, inference, conference, instance, confidence, providence, residence, expense, recompense, encumbrance, remembrance, acceptance.

Diference, diferent, indiferent, diferently, indiferently. Given, giving, forgiven, forgiving. Objective, subjective. Objects, subjects, principles, improves, values, forms, things, numbers, languages, represents, remarks, generals, advantages, enlarges, pleasures, questions.

Conformable, remarkable, valuable, questionable, objectionable, improvable, pleasurable.

Objectively, subjectively, instructively, distinctively. Principally, uniformly, remarkably, generally, gentlemanly, unqestionably, wholly, largely.

Formed, informed, deformed, questioned, unquestioned, objected, subjected, unprincipled, improved, valued, acknowledged, represented, outgeneraled, numbered, unnumbered, remarked.

Objecting, subjecting, improving, valuing, forming, reforming, informing, numbering, acknowledging, representing, remarking, questioning, willing.

NATIONAL CHARACTER. — *The loss of a firm national character, or the degradation of a nation's honor, is the inevitable prelude to her destruction. Behold the once proud fabric of the Roman empire, an empire carrying* its arts and arms into every part of the eastern continent. Where is her splendor, her welth, her power, her glory? Extinguisht forever. Her moldering temples, the mornful vestiges of her former grandeur, afford a shelter to her muttering monks. Where ar her statesmen, her sages, her philosophers, her orators, her generals? Go to their solitary tombs, and inquire. She lost her national character, and her destruction followed. Citizens will lose their respect and confidence in our government if it does not extend over them the shield of an honorable national character. Corruption will creep in, and sharpen party animosity. Ambitius leaders will seize upon the favorable moment. The mad enthusiasm for revolution will call into action the irritated spirit of our nation, and civil war must follow. The swords of our countrymen may yet glitter on our mountains: their blood may yet crimson our plains.

Such the warning voice of all antiquity, the example of all republics, proclaim may be our fate.—MAXCY.

WRITING EXERCISE EIGHTEENTH.

Wilful, wilfully, formality, numberless, phonographic, tachygraphic, generalissimo, whence, whilst, largest, advantageous.
Unobjectionable, unsubjected, unprincipled, unimproved, uniform, uniformity, unacknowledged, unrepresented, ungentlemanly. Disadvantageously. Anything, nothing. Altogether, also, although, always, whoever, whose, whom, however. Give, given, giver, giving, forgiven, unforgiven, forgiveness. Difficulties, signify, significant, insignificancy. Practicable, impracticable, unpracticed, respect,

respectful, respectfully, respectively, irrespective. Outrage, outrageous, useful, usefully, usefulness.

Well-being, well-wisher, many-sided, word-forms, ever-enduring, never-ending, heavy-laden, fellow-citizens, fellow-countrymen, pleasure-seeker, never-to-be-forgotten.

LABOR.—*Labor is life; from the inmost hart of the worker rises his God-given force, the sacred celestial life-essence, breathed into him by Almighty God. Doubt of whatever kind can be ended by action only. Older than all preached gospels was this unpreacht, inarticulate, but ineradicable, forever-enduring gospel—work, and therein hav well-being. All true work is sacred. In all true work, wer it but true hand-labor, ther is somthing of divinenes. Labor wide as the world has its summit in heven.*

Who art thou that complainest of thy life of toil? Complain not. Look up, my wearied brother; see thy fellow-workmen there in God's eternity; surviving there, they alone surviving,—sacred bands of the immortals. Even in the weak human memory they survive so long, as saints and heroes,—they alone surviving,—peopling alone the immesured solitudes of time. To thee Heven, tho severe, is not unkind. Heven is kind as a noble mother,—as that Spartan mother, saying, while she gave her son his shield, "With it, my son, or upon it." Thou, too, shalt return home in honor,—in honor to thy far-distant home. Doubt it not, if, in the battle, thou but keep thy shield.—THOMAS CARLYLE.

OUR COUNTRY'S FUTURE.—*Unborn ages and visions of glory crowd upon my soul, the realization of all which, however, is in the hands and good plesure of Almihty God; but, under his divine blesing, it will be dependent* on the character and the virtues of ourselves and our posterity. If classical history has bin found to be, is now, and shal continue to be, the concomitant of free institutions, and of popular eloquence, what a field is opening to us for another Heroditus, another Thucidides, and another Livy. And let me say, gentlemen, that if we and our posterity shal be true to the Christian religion, — if we and they shal liv always in the fear of God, and shal respect his commandments, — if we and they shall maintain just moral sentiments, and such conscientius convictions of duty as shal controll the hart and life, — we may hav the hihest hopes of the future fortunes of our country; and if we maintain those institutions of government, and that political union, exceeding all praise as much as it does all former examples of political associations, we may be sure of one thing, — that while our country furnishes materials for a thousand masters of the historic art, it will afford no topic for a Gibbon, — it will hav no Decline and Fall. It will go on prospering, and to prosper. But if we and our posterity reject religius instruction and authority, violate the rules of eternal justice, trifle with the injunctions of morality, and recklesly destroy the political constitution which holds us together, no man can tel how sudden a catastrophe may overwhelm us that shal bury all our glory in profound obscurity. Shud that catastrophe happen, let it have no history. Let the horrible narrativ never be written. Let its fate be like the lost books of Livy, which no human eye shall ever read; or the missing Pleiad, of which no man can ever kno more than that it is lost, and lost forever. — DANIEL WEBSTER.

CHAPTER IX.

PHRASE SIGNS.

93. *a.* The general principles determining the use of phrase-signs are the same as those given in the first style of the art. The student will do well to review Chapter IX of the Elements as an introduction to this chapter.

The phrases of the Note-Taker's style differ from those in the simpler style principally in the brevity of the word-forms of which they are composed.

b. A large number of very valuable phrase-signs may be made by joining the simple word-signs together, as explained on page 33.

SPEC.—Other phrases may be formed in a similar way, like the following: *of-the, of-all, all-of, of-that, of-which, of-these, of-this, of-some, of-many, in-no, in-some.* (R. L., sec. 110.) See, also, the phrase-signs given in Table A, at the end of this chapter.

94. The use of the word-signs joined in phrases is guided by the same principles as those already given for the joining of letters into word-forms. Yet, the following specifications may aid the

writer in some cases of doubt in securing good forms for phrases.

SPEC. 1. *a.*—The word-sign ɔ, *in,* is written ᴖ before ⌒, as *in-me, in-my, in-many.* (R. L., sec. 111.)

b. The word *in* may be written in full more easily than by the word-sign in cases where the ‿ is needed for a connecting stroke, as in *in-a, in-one, in-what.* (R. L., sec. 120.)

2. The word-sign ᴗ, *have,* may either begin or end a phrase, or stand between other signs, as *have-I, I-have, have-they, they-have, I-have-not, we-have-seen.* But it will be well to avoid using the ᴗ for *have* before), as it would be possible in that case to read it *ad.* Hence, such phrases as *I-have-ventured* should be divided into *I-have ventured;* but the phrase *I-have-advised,* where the *have* precedes the *ad,* may be used. (R. L., sec., 111, *b* and *c.*)

3. The word-sign ⁄, *all,* though generally struck downward, may be struck upward wherever the upward form is more convenient. The upward form will be preferred generally before |, |, ʹ (con and com), ‿, ᴗ, ⁄, ⁄, ⌒, ⌒, as in the phrases *all-persons, all-conditions, all-nations, all-senses, all-works, all-hearts, all-ages.* (R. L., sec. 112.)

4. *a.* The word-sign ⁄, *of,* is written upward generally in phrases, but may be written downward when necessary to form a convenient angle, as in *of-these, of-recent-times, of-commendation, of-sufficient, of-them, of-the-same.* (R. L., sec. 113.)

b. When *of* precedes a word commencing with the vowel ⌒ (ŏ), as in the phrase *of-opportunities,* the vowel is displaced by the word-sign and omitted, as in *in-the-midst, of-opportunities, for-usefulness.* (R. L., sec. 114.) But in some cases of this kind the /, *of*, may be added to the preceding word.

5. The tick for *the* takes the place of the initial vowel / (ŏ) in such phrases as *the-opposition, the-occurrence, the-obstacles;* but if it is desired to retain the vowel, the tick may be added to the preceding word, as in *on the occurrence of this festival.* (R. L., sec. 119.)

6. The word *us* may be written by the circle in phrases where the ⌒ is inconvenient, as *It-will-afford-us-much-pleasure; they-will-send-us-supplies; of-us, some-of-us.* (R. L., sec. 114, *b*.)

7. It is better to preserve the word-sign ⌊, *they*, in its proper form, and to change other words to conform to it when necessary, as in the phrases *they-are, they-may, they-may-be.* The word *them* may be written like *they-may* if unavoidable; but it will be generally easy to retain its proper form, as in *let-them, set-them, for-them, hear-them.* (R. L., sec. 115.)

8. The word-sign ⌐, *though*, is invariable: so, also, are the signs - *who*, ⁄ *how*, ⌣ *on* and *own*, and ⟋ *we*.

Ex.—*Though-they, though-these, though-this, though-we, who-is, how-is, on-us, their-own, we-know.* (R. L., sec. 116.)

9. The word-sign ⌐, *may*, is written either upward or downward. It is sometimes made heavy to represent the phrase *may-be*. The words *you* and *he* are sometimes written with other signs than those given in the table. (See sec. 96.)

10. The word-sign ⁄, *are*, may be written either upward or downward, as *are-they, they-are, are-we, we-are, who-are.* (R. L., sec. 117.)

11. The word-sign ⌐, *will*, may be written either up-

ward or downward, as in *they-will, who-will, we-will-endeavor.* (R. L., sec. 118.)

95. The word-sign ⌒ may be written for *you* whenever this word follows) or); or precedes ⌒, as in the phrases *if-you, love-you, you-may, you-must, if-you-must.* (R. L., sec. 121.)

SPEC.—Since these phrases do not distinguish between *ye* and *you*, wherever it is thought sufficiently important to make this distinction, the ⌣ must be used for *you*, as in the first style. But the distinction will be obvious enough in most cases from the sense of the writing.

96. The tick for *h* may be used for *he* in many phrases, and the sign ⌒ may be used for *he-may.*

Ex.—He-is, he-thinks, he-sees, he-lives, he-saves, he-may-be. (R. L., sec. 122, *a.*)

This tick and hook may also be used in the midst of a phrase, as in *if-he-was, for-he-may, if-he-will, when-he-is.* (R. L., sec. 122, *b.*)

SPEC. 1.—The use of the tick for *he* is considerably extended in the reporting style, but it will be better to limit it in this style to phrases of frequent occurrence, and where its use is not liable to be confounded with the *con* and *com*, or the word-sign ⸝, *of.*

The *con* and *com* occur frequently before —, —,), and), hence it will be well generally to avoid the use of the tick for *he* before these letters. Yet the phrases *he-did* and *he-did-not* are used.

2. The tick for *he* will be distinguished from the word-sign ╱, *of*, in many cases, because it is struck downward, while the ╱, *of*, is struck upward; but before ⟋ and ⟍ the ╱, *he*, is struck upward, and may be mistaken for *of*. So, also, in a few other cases the signs for *of* and *he* may be confounded. Yet no real difficulty need result from this, for only in very rare cases will the phrases themselves be indeterminate, as will be seen in the following examples: *he-had, of-what, he-was, of-wisdom, if-he-should, many-of-them, he-seems.* (R. L., sec. 123.)

97. *a.* The circle for *as* may be made twice its usual size in such phrases as *as-some-suppose, as-specified.*

b. The ⌒ may be halved for the phrase *as-it*, and trebled in the phrases *as-there-is* and *as-there-may-be.* (R. L., sec. 124, *a.*)

SPEC.—The following phrases may be used with the halved or trebled ⌒: *as-it-is, as-it-was, as-it-were, as-there-are, as-there-were, who-is-there,* and some others. (R. L., sec. 124, *b.*)

98. *a.* The word-signs ⌒ *so*, ⟍ *though*, ⟋ *may*, ⌣ *when*, ∫ *while*, and ⟍ *will* may be trebled to add the expletive *there*, as in the phrases *so-there-is, though-there-is, may-there-be, when-there-is, while-there-is, will-there-be.* (R. L., sec. 125.)

b. In analogy with these lengthened signs, the

⌣ of the termination *ing* may be trebled to add the pronoun *their* as in the phrases *desiring-their, loving-their, giving-their.* (R. L., sec. 126.)

Spec.—A few other cases of lengthened curves will be found in Table E. The student should observe that the ⌣ only is lengthened to add *their*, while the other lengthened curves, except ⟍, add *there* only. The ⟍ is lengthened to add *there* and *other*.

Rem. 1.—Phonographers add *there, their,* and *other* indiscriminately by means of lengthened curves. Whatever may be the advantage of this in the reporting style, the demands of the Note-Taker's style will, it is believed, be best served by the limitations given above.

Rem. 2.—The use of the trebled ⌣ to represent *ngr* in the words *anger, linger,* &c. (see sec. 51) will not interfere with its use in the phrases mentioned in this section.

SHORTENED PHRASES.

99. As some word-forms are contracted by means of the general principles of contraction, and others by the omission of one or more radical letters, so phrase-signs may be contracted regularly, as in the preceding sections, by the use of shortened or lengthened characters, &c., or more or less irregularly by means of omissions or elisions. These omissions cannot be classified in this style, for they are purposely limited to a

CHAPTER IX. 153

few phrases of frequent occurrence, and can be best learned from the tables which follow.

Spec. 1.—The vowel ⌣ is used for *at* in the phrases *at-all-events, at-first, at-last, at-large, at-length, at-once*. (R. L., sec. 127 and Table B.)

This contracted form for *at* should be strictly limited, as otherwise it might be confounded with *have* or *ad*.

2. The word *and* is omitted in the phrases *for-ever-and ever* and *more-and-more*.

3. The word *the* is omitted in the phrase-signs *for-the-most-part, in-the-name-of, in-the-first-place, in-the-last-place*. (R. L., sec. 128.)

4. The phrases *for-instance, from-time-to-time, in-connection-with, in-proportion-to, more-than, on-either-hand, as-much-as*, and others found in Tables B and C, represent each some mode of shortening adapted to these special cases alone. (R. L., sec. 129.)

100. The words *because, can, for, from, has, his, I, it, much, not, only, or, when, will*, and *your* may also be contracted in certain phrases, as given in Table D.

Spec. 1.—The signs for *cannot* and *could-not* use the *n* hook on the halved ╲. These forms may be employed in longer phrases in which these words occur, as *I-cannot-do, he-could-not-be, we-cannot-think, they-could-not-do*. (R. L., sec. 130.)

2. The word *it* is added to the signs for *if, because, when*, and *while* by shortening the), ⌢, ⌣, and ╱.

So, also, *its* is implied by adding the circle to the shortened form.

3. The ⋁ drops its second stroke in *I-may, I-am*, and so also in *I-must-be, I-mean, I-meant*. (R. L., sec. 131, *a*.)

REM.—The ⋁ does not drop its *first* stroke in phrases. The ⁄ is used for *he* or *of* instead of *I* in the commencement of phrases. Phonographers should take a note of this, as the first stroke of the ⋁ has been dropped in that system.

4. *a*. The words *his* and *has* are contracted into the circle, or into a circle and tick, as will be seen in the phrases *in-his, of-his, he-has, it-has-been,* and others. (Table D.)

b. Generally the tick is struck up in *has* and down in *his;* but the construction of the phrase may make it necessary in some cases to reverse this direction.

c. The following examples will sufficiently illustrate the use of *his* and *has* in phrases: *with-his, to-his, on-his, it-has, it-has-not, has-had, has-been, has-not, has-done, he-has-had.* (R. L., sec. 131, *b*.)

5. The use or omission of the ⸝ and ⸍ in phrases containing the words *from* and *for* need not be definitely limited. But where the use of these letters is not necessary either for convenience of joining or for distinguishing the phrases, they may be omitted.

Ex.—For-this, for-these, for-us, from-us, for-me, from-me, from-which, for-many-reasons. (R. L., sec. 131, *c*.)

6. The use of ⌒ for *it*, as given in the phrase *it-has-been*, should be limited in this style to the cases following. The ⌒ may be used for *it* in the commencement of a phrase—

a. Whenever it is followed by *has*, written ⸝⸍, *it-has*.

Ex. — It-has-not, it-has-done, it-has-come, &c. (R. L., sec. 132, *a*.)

CHAPTER IX.   155

b. When followed by *had*, written ⌢, *it-had*, as in the phrases *it-had-been, it-had-not.* (R. L., sec. 132, *b.*)

c. When followed by *is, may, must, might*, as in the phrases *it-is, it-is-not, it-may-seem, it-must-be, it-might-be.*

d. In the phrases *it-ought-to-be, it-ought-not-to-be.* (R. L., sec. 132, *c* and *d.*)

7. The phrases *it-will* and *you-will* are written with the large-hook signs ⊂ and ∪ The former of these signs is used also in word-forms, and the latter is used in the terminations *ual* and *ually.* These phrases are used freely in all connections, as in *it-will-do, as-it-will-be, I-hope-it-will, as-you-will, for-you-will, where-you-will.* (R. L., sec. 133.)

8. The letter ∪ is written for *your*, as well as *you*, without danger of confusion.

Ex.— *Your-own, your-own-selves, yourself, your-duty;* but the ╱ may be added when necessary for joining, as in *your-pleasure, your-friends.* (R. L., sec. 134.)

101. *a.* The phrases *at-it, at-which, by-it, by-which, do-it* (or *done-it*), *have-it* (or *have-to*), *in-it, may-it, of-it, on-it, to-it, with-it, within-it, without-it*, as given in Table E and R. L., 135, need little comment. After —, ⌢, ⌒, and ' (*of*) the *it* is written in full. This is merely for convenience, as it is difficult to add — to these letters without some connecting stroke.

b. The words *at, in,* and *out,* when they follow a verb, as in the phrases *laugh-at, come-in,* &c.,

may unite with either the preceding or following word as may be more convenient.

Ex.—*Laugh-at, look-at, come-in, go-in, go-out, set-out, they-laughed, at him, let-us-go, into-(the-) house.* (R. L., sec. 136.)

102. *a.* In the tables which follow examples are given of the principal forms of contracted phrases which are explained in the preceding sections. They should be thoroughly mastered by the student, and the additional examples given in the reading lessons added to them. When this is done, the student will be prepared to apply the same principles to the phrases given in the writing lessons.

Spec.—It is expected that the student will learn to form phrases for himself freely wherever it is convenient to do so. But in doing this he will do well to bear in mind the following general directions.

a. He should form shortened and irregular phrases only in accordance with the models given in the tables and the reading lessons; and most persons will find those given quite sufficient for their use without adding to this class of signs.

b. Of the regular and simple phrases, which consist of joining two or more words without any change in the words joined, new ones may be made at convenience, but they should not be too long. Simplicity is essential to speed. Most phrases should consist of only two words, but if they are very short, three words may be joined into a phrase.

c. The particles, — prepositions, conjunctions, pronouns, and adverbs, — with the auxiliary verbs, form the closest connection in sense with one another and with other words, and should generally be joined to the words to which they belong. Such are the following words: *and, as, but, by, for, from, if, in, of, on, or, to, under, unto, with, without. All, each, he, her, his, I, it, its, many, me, my, one, our, she, some, such, their, they, these, this, those. Am, are, art, be, been, can, could, did, do, done, had, has, have, is, may, might, must, shall, should, were, will, would. Never, no, not, same, still, than, then, until,* and some other words.

Rem. 1. — Most of the words given in this list have been introduced previously in connection with the principles of contraction which are applied to phrases. The writer must be familiar with them as written separately, and as modified in the shortened phrases.

Rem. 2. — The use of phrases in the Reading Lessons should be carefully studied. The selection from the first chapter of Job, given at the close of the illustrations of shortened phrases, on page 15, will afford a good model for imitation in regard to the length of phrases for general use.

Rem. 3. — In studying the following tables, the student should refer to the explanation of the principles given in the preceding sections. These forms should be rendered so familiar as to be written with the greatest rapidity, and with a fair degree of accuracy.

SIMPLE PHRASE-SIGNS. — TABLE A.

⌒ in the,   ⌒• of that,
⌒ in this,   ⌒ of which,
⌒ in that,   ⁄ of all,
⌒ in no,   ⁄ of the,
⌒ in some,   ⌒ of some,
⌒ in me,   ⌒ of any,
⌒ who will,   ⌒ how is,
⌒ who is,   ⌒ how could,
⌒ who would,   ⌒ how sure,
⌒ who had,   ⌒ we are,
⌒ have we,   ⌒ are we,
⌒ have I,   ⌒ were we,
⌒ have they,   ⌒ we were,
⌒ all of,   ⌒ with some,
⌒ all the,   ⌒ with us.

CHAPTER IX.

BRIEF PHRASE-SIGNS. — TABLE B.

	as it were,		in consequence of,
	at all events,		in proportion to,
	at first,		in respect to,
	at last,		in reference to,
	at length,		in the mean time,
	at once,		in the name of,
	by chance,		in the first place,
	by no means,		in the last place,
	forever,		in the second place,
	forever and ever,		less than,
	for instance,		let us,
	for the purpose of,		more and more,
	for the most part,		more frequently,
	from time to time,		more or less,
	in accordance with,		more than,
	in connection with,		must be,

TABLE B — CONTINUED.

~	no more,		the other,
	now and then,		with respect to,
	once more,		with reference to,
	on account of,		western States,
	on no account,		eastern States,
	on one account,		southern States,
	on either hand,		U. S.,
	on the other hand		U. S. of Am.

SPECIAL PHRASES. — TABLE C.

	as is,		as far as,
	is as,		as much as,
	as a,		as some say,
	as in,		is there,
	as it,		there is,
	as to,		one or two,
	as if,		two or three.

CHAPTER IX.

TABLE D.

˘	cannot,	✓	I am, I may,
ˋ	could not,	ə	in his,
⟩	for this,	⸱	of his,
⟩⌒	for he is,	⌒	he has,
⟩⌢	for he was,	⟩⌒	if he has,
⟩⌒	for it is,	⟨	it has been,
⟩⚬	for its own sake,	⌒	how much,
⟩	from it,	⌒	the only way,
⟩	if it is,	⟩⌒	this or that,
⟩	because it is,	⌒	right or wrong,
⌣	when it is,	⟨	it will be,
⟋	while it is,	⟨	you will be,
⟩	if you,	⌒	you are,
⌣	though you may,	⟝	yours truly.

REM. — For the explanation of the phrases in this Table see sections 99 and 100.

TABLE E.

	as there are,		at it,
	as there is not,		by it,
	if there are, if there is, if there is not,		do it, done it,
	in another,		have it,
	in neither,		in it,
	in their,		may it,
	though there are, the other way,		of it,
			on it,
	when there are, while there are, will there be, doing their,		to it,
			with it,
	giving their,		within it,
	knowing their,		without it,
	are such,		in you,
	of such,		in your,
	with such,		let there be.

CHAPTER IX.

WRITING EXERCISE NINETEENTH.

The phrases are separated by commas. Words not separated by commas or periods are to be joined.

In me, in my, in this, in that, in them, in their, in those, in this case, in those days, in such a way, in some way.

Who can, who could, who will, who would, who shall, who should, who have, who have been, who had been, who may be.

Have they, have you, have we, have I, have been, have not, have not been.

All of, all the, all of the, all men, all times.

Of this, if that, of which, of me, of no, of any, of some, of the, of their, of all, of which it is.

How far, how soon, how is, how is it, how could, how can, how easy, how sure, how strange.

We have, we would, we can, we could, we shall, we should, we are, we were. Were we, were you, were they, were this. With it, with that, with this, with which, with some, with me, with him, with us, with words, with God.

They were, they shall, they shall be, they shall have, they know, they wish. Though this, though some, though certain.

May we, may they, may you, may have, may I, may not, may not be, may have been.

On this, on that, on this account, on that account, on no account, on one account, on my account, on me, on some, on which, on all.

Are we, are you, are they, are they sure, are not.

You have, you shall, you know, you need not, you can, you could, you can be, you have been. He can, he shall, he knows, he loves, he lives.

Immortality of the Soul.— Among many excellent arguments for the immortality of the soul, ther is one drawn from the perpetual progress of the soul to its perfection, without a possibility of ever arriving at it.

How can it ever enter into the tho'ts of man that the soul, which is capable of such immense perfections, and of receiving new improvements to all eternity, shall fall away into nothing almost as soon as it is created? Are such abilities made to no purpose? A brute arrives at a point of perfection that he can never pas; in a few years he has all the endowments he is capable of; and wer he to liv ten thousand more, wud be the same thing he is at present. But a man can never hav taken in his full mesure of knolege. He has not time to subdue his passions, establish his soul in virtue, and come up to the perfection of his nature, before he is hurried off the stage.

Wud an infinitely wise being make such glorius creatures for so mean a purpose? Can he delite in the production of such abortiv intelligences, such short-lived reasonable beings? Wud he giv us talents that are not to be exerted, and capacities that are never to be gratified?

How can we find that wisdom which shines throo all his works in the formation of man without looking on this world as only a nursery for the next, and believing that the several generations of rational creatures which rise up and disappear in such quick successions ar only to receiv their first rudiments of existence here, and afterwards to be transplanted into a more frendly climate, where they may spred and flurish to all eternity.— ADDISON.

CHAPTER IX.

WRITING EXERCISE TWENTIETH.

The phrases are separated by commas.

As it were, as it was, as it will be, as it has been, as it should be. At all events, at all times, at first, at last, at length, at large, at once, at one time.

By chance, by some means, by the same means, by no means, by all means. For ever and ever, for instance, for the most part, for the purpose of, for the sake of, from time to time, from this time, from that time, from ancient times.

In accordance with, in account with, in connection with, in consequence of, in many cases, in many places, in proportion to, in reference to, in regard to, in respect to, in the mean time, in the name of, in the first place, in the last place, in the next place, in the second place, in the third place. In any way, in no way, in some way, in every way.

Less than, let us, let us not, let us see, let us look, let us come, let us suppose.

More and more, moreover, more or less, more frequently, more closely, more than, more than that, more than this, must not, must be, must have (the — is retained in *must have*), *must come. No more, no more than, no less than this, now and then.*

On account of, on account of this, on no account, on some accounts, on either hand, on the one hand, on the other hand, once more.

The other, the other way, the other day, in the other, on the other. With respect to, with reference to, with respect to this, with respect to that, with reference to this.

Western States, in the western States, in the eastern

States, in the southern States, in the United States of America.

LETTERS.—G. D. MITCHELL.—*Blessed be letters! They ar the monitors, they ar also the comforters, and they are the only true heart-talkers. Your speech, and their speech, ar conventional; they are molded by circumstances; they ar suggested by the observation, remark, and influence of the parties to whom the speaking is addrest, or by whom it may be overherd. Your truest tho't is modified half throo its utterance by a look, a sign, a smile, or a sneer. But it is not so with letters: there you ar with only the soulless pen, and the snow-white, virgin paper. Your soul is mesuring itself by itself, and saying its own sayings: ther ar no sneers to modify its utterance, no scowl to scare: nothing is present but you and your tho't.*

Oh, the glory, the freedom, the passion of a letter! It is worth all the lip-talk of the world. Do you say it is studied, made up, acted, reherst, contrived, artistic? Let me see it, then; let me run it over; tell me age, sex, circumstances, and I wil tel you if it be studied or real,—if it be the merest lip-slang put into words, or hart-talk blazing on the paper.

*Ar we not creatures of tho't and passion? Is anything about us more ernest than that same tho't and passion? Is ther anything more real, more characteristic of that great and dim destiny to which we ar born, and which may be written down in that terrible word—*FOREVER! *Let those who will, then, sneer at what in their wisdom they call untruth, at what is false, because it has no material presence: this duz not create falsity,—wud to Heven that it did.*

CHAPTER X.

THE TACHYGRAPHIC NOMENCLATURE.

102. *a.* In giving oral instruction in Tachygraphy, it is often desirable to speak of the compound and complex signs that enter into the word-forms as well as the simple letters. In order to do this intelligibly, it is necessary that the teacher and pupil become familiar with some system of naming the signs.

b. Names for the simple letters are given in connection with the alphabet, on page 43 of the Elements; and the names of the compounds of the L, R, and S-series are given in the following table of the compound signs. (See p. 170.)

103. *a.* In spelling Tachygraphically, it will be found convenient to *name* each *stem* by a distinctive name. A full-sized, half-length, double, or treble-length sign, with such circles or hooks as may be attached to it, forms a *stem*.

b. Stems which take a vowel after them may be properly distinguished from those which do not admit a vowel after them: the former may be regarded as *open*, and the latter as *closed*. To make this distinction appear in the names, it is convenient to name stems which take a vowel after them with open syllables, and those which do not take a vowel after them with closed syllables.

Ex.— ⌠ *bla*, ⌠ *bra*, ⌠ *spe*, ⌠ *spra*, ⌠ *qua*, when initial; and ⌠ *bul*, ⌠ *bur*, ⌠ *spur*, when final.

104. Contracted signs should designate in their names either that use to which they are put in the word spelled, or that use to which they are more frequently and properly applied.

Spec. 1.— The double circle may be called *sus*, as in ⌠ *sus-pe*. On the end of a stem it may be named *ses*, as ⌠ *penses*.

2. The half-lengths may be named by writing the short *ĕ* before the shortened letter, or introducing it before the added *d* or *t*, thus, ⌠ *ept* or *pet*, \ *ekt* or *ket*. When the heavy signs are halved, the name will end in *d*, as *ebd* or *bed*.

3. When a circle is attached to the half-length, the combination may be named in a similar manner, as in ⌠ *sept* or *spet*. So, also, with the double circle, as in ⌠ *sus ept*.

4. *a.* When a circle ends the character, it is named as in the table,— ⌠ *eps*, ⌠ *ex*, &c. When halved, these signs read ⌠ *epts* or *pets*, ⌠ *ekts* or *kets*.

b. When a hook or circle commences the sign, and a circle ends it, it is named in a similar manner, as in ⌠ *plens*, ⌠ *pres* or *pars*, ⌠ *spes* or *seps*, ⌠ *spres*.

5. Final hooks are treated like the final circle, and the

letter or letters they represent end the name of the stem on which they occur.

Ex.— ⌡ *pen,* ⌡ *spren,* ∫ *spen,* ⌊ *peshn,* ⌡ *pef* or *pev.*

6. *a.* The lengthened curves are named by adding *tr* and *thr* to the name of the letter lengthened, as ⌣ *enter,* ⌣ *enther,* &c.

b. The trebled ⌣ is named *ingger* when it implies *gr,* and *ingther* when it implies *their.*

7. The names of all prefixes and affixes will be found in the tables of these signs. In spelling, the prefix or affix may be named in all cases except where a letter is used as an affix: in that case, the letter retains its own name, as in ⌣⌡ *in-enter-en-ya, intercommunion.*

REM.—The following tables give the names of the principal modifications of the straight stems, as illustrated in the letter |, and the names of the compounds of the L, R, and S-series. The names of the letters not given will be easily understood from the illustrations given in this section.

105. Vocals may be named separately, as in the alphabet, and the long vocals can be named in no other way; but the short vocals may be named in connection with the following consonant, as ⌣ *ac* for *ă-Ka.*

Stems ending in vowel-hooks are named as they are pronounced, as → *dy,* → *ty,* \ *că.*

106. The signs used in phrases may be named as the same signs are named in word-forms; but if any signs occur in the phrases which do

not occur in the word-forms, they should have distinctive names.

107. Students may be exercised to advantage in spelling; but a few exercises will suffice to render the method of spelling entirely familiar to an intelligent class.

The following examples will serve as farther illustrations of the names of Tachygraphic stems: *ma-a-en-es-pra-ing*, mainspring; *la-ef-ty*, lofty; *pe-o-est*, post; *sest-ma*, system; *eps-est* or *pe-sest*, possest; *es-ste*, assessed; *clet*, called; *ef-i-later*, filter; *ra-end-ar*, render; *ra-ender*, render; *ka-o-enter* or *ka-onter*, counter; *ă-enther* or *anther*, another; *anther-pe-la-o-gy*, anthropology.

con-ste-te-te, constitute; *contra-ve-e-en*, contravene; *im-ma-ra-tel*, immortal; *in-shel*, initial; *in-bred*, inbred; *in-sect*, insect; *obshn*, objection; *opshn*, option; *dis-pe-a* or *dis-pa*, dissipation.

NAMES OF COMPOUND SIGNS.

꜓	bra or ber,	꜑	bla or bel,
꜒	pra or per,	꜐	pla or pel,
↘	gra or ger,	↘	gla or gel,
↘	cra or ker,	↘	cla or kel,
—	dra or der,	⊂	del,
—	tra or ter,	⊂	tel,
)	ver,	⌒	vel,
)	fra or fer,	⌒	fla or fel,
∕	zher,	⌒	zhel,
∕	shra or sher,	⌒	shel,
⌒	ther,	⌒	nel,
⌒	thra or ther,	⌒	sne or sen,
⌣	ner,	⌣ ⌒	sla, sle, sel,
⌣	wha,	⌣	swa,
꜑	spe or sep,	⌒	māz, emz,
↘	ske or sek,	⌣	ens or enz,
∘—	ste or set,	⌣	engz,
)	sfe or sef,	⌒	lāz, els, or elz,
⌒ ⌒	sma, sme, sem,	⌒	ers or erz,

CHAPTER X.

NAMES OF COMPOUND SIGNS — CONTINUED.

eps,
epses,
pens,
penses,
pen,
pen,
peshn,
pef or pev,
peshns,
pefs,
seps or spes,
spens,
spenses,
spen,
speshns,

spra,
sus-pe,
sus-pra,
pet or ept,
spet or sept,
sus-pet,
spret,
pets,
pents,
ples,
preses,
sus-pens,
pren,
spren,
spreshn.

CHAPTER X. 173

WRITING EXERCISE TWENTY-FIRST.

Exercise on the Use of the Names of the Signs.

Be-pe-te-sme, in-ka-ma, Ka-a-em, de-smé, de-sla-ish-en, sla-ve-dent, con-tent, con-ekt, com-p-en-d, com-peshn, con-tra-acshn, contra-dy-keshn, contra-dy-ekt, in-ef-te-yashn, con-gra-at-yulashn, com-and, com-end, con-si-end, inter-ef-e-rens. Magni-te-de, or-na-ment, scra-ment-el.

> *Through knowledge we behold the world's creation,*
> *How in his cradle first he fondled was,*
> *And judge of Nature's cunning operation,*
> *How things she formed of a formles mass.*
> *By knowledge we do learn ourselves to know,*
> *And what to man and what to God we owe;*
> *From hence we mount aloft unto the sky,*
> *And look into the crystal firmament.*
> *There we behold the Heaven's great hierarchy,*
> *The stars' pure light, the spheres' swift movement,*
> *The spirits and intelligences fair,*
> *And angels waiting on the Almighty's chair;*
> *And there with humble mind, and high in light,*
> *The Eternal Maker's majesty we view,—*
> *His love, his truth, his glory, and his might,*
> *And mercy more than mortal man can view.*
> *Oh, Sovereign Lord, oh, sovereign happines!*
> *To see Thee and thy mercy measureles!*
> *Such happines have they that do embrace*
> *The precepts of thy heavenly discipline;*
> *But shame and sorrow and acursed case*
> *Have they that scorn the school of arts divine,*
> *And banish me, which do possess the skill*
> *To make men heavenly wise through humbled will.*
> EDMUND SPENCER.

MYSTERY.—*In loveliness of form, or of moral character, or of the material creation, it is that which is most* veiled which is most beautiful. The mysteries of the heart and of nature are the delight of the intellect, the soul, and the eyes. It seems as if the Creator had drawn a shadow over whatever he has made most delicate and most divine to, by its secrecy, heighten our aspirations after it, and to soften its lustre from our gaze, in a manner as he has placed lids over our eyes to temper the light when its impression is too great upon them. Valleys are the mysteries of landscapes; the more we long to penetrate them, the more they try to wind and bury and hide themselves. Mist is to mountains what illusion is to love, — it elevates them. Mystery hovers over everything here below, and solemnizes all things to the eyes and to the heart.

IMMORTALITY. — When I think that I am to outlive the sun and the stars, that I am to be freed from the limited influence of time, that ages on ages will roll over me without touching the youthful vigor of my soul, that mansions of light and purity are prepared for me by the holy being who once dwelt on earth, that I shall live there in closer intimacy with God than with an earthly parent, that saints and apostles will be my companions, Jesus the Redeemer will be my brother, I am oppressed with the responsibility of immortality. And to the hands of each one of us is committed a spirit to be fitted for this endless, glorious life. The spirit is ourself. Its culture is the development of its every faculty.

> *Afar behind expression hides*
> *The thing to be expressed.*
> *Deep underneath all that we do,*
> *And all we seem,*
> *Lies what we feel;*
> *And what we feel, we are*

CHAPTER XI.

ANALOGY AND EUGRAPHY.

108. Allusion has previously been made to certain general principles, or laws, that have an influence upon word-forms, and which, running through the entire field of word-forms, bind them together into one system. These principles may be considered, so far as is necessary for practical purposes, under two general divisions, the laws of analogy, and the laws of eugraphy.

109. Analogy consists in a similarity in certain respects between things which are in other respects different. When applied to the outlines of words in Tachygraphy, analogy consists in writing such portions of two or more words as are alike in sound in the same manner, and such portions as are similar in a similar manner.

SPEC. 1.—The nature of the principle stated in this section will be seen in the following examples:—

In the words in*gress*, e*gress*, di*gress*, con*gress*, re*gress*, trans*gress*, di*gress*ing, trans*gress*ors, the root *gress*, which is put in italics, appears without change. The law of analogy is observed here in the common spelling; but if the first word was spelled in*gress*, the second e*gres*, the third di*greas*, the fourth con*grace*, and so on, this law would be broken.

2. In Tachygraphy, the original root-form is retained so far as possible in all the derivations. The principle may be traced in those derived from the word-signs, and elsewhere.

The word ⟩— *form*, for instance, remains unchanged throughout a list of over a hundred derived words. (See section 90.)

But this principle applies to all classes of words, and to all parts of words. As the same sound is written by the same sign, so the same combination of sounds is written by the same combination of signs, unless some other law interferes to effect an exception to the rule.

3. Such exceptions do occur, and not infrequently, but no exception should be admitted without sufficient reason. Some exceptions are given in the end of the following section.

THE LAWS OF ANALOGY.

110. The principal features of the agreement of word-forms with similar word-forms are included in these rules.

a. Derivative words are written in analogy with their primatives.

b. Compound words are written in analogy both with the simple words from which they are formed, and with other compounds formed by uniting any of their parts.

c. In all classes of words the same combination of letters are written, so far as possible, in the same manner.

Spec. 1. *a.*—The first rule applies especially to the derivative word-signs, and to that large class of words formed by means of the addition of prefixes and affixes. These derived forms are, for the most part, regularly formed. A given stem remains unchanged throughout the entire list of derivative forms, and even the prefix and affix signs have some analogy to the signs from which they are derived.

b. The words ⟨⟩, *compress*, and ⟨⟩ *impress*, for example, are written analogically in having the root *press* written with the same form in both words; but the words ⟨⟩ and ⟨⟩ are analogous only in regard to the prefix which is common to them both.

c. Some exceptions to the laws of analogy will be noticed, such, for instance, as ⟨⟩, *larger*, and ⟨⟩, *useful*, from ⟨⟩ and ⟨⟩.

2. Word-forms remain so constant in outline that they suffer change very infrequently in forming compounds. Hence the 2nd rule admits of very few exceptions, and these may be regarded as special contractions.

Ex.— ⟨sign⟩ *overwhelm*, and ⟨sign⟩ *elsewhere*.

3. The third rule embraces a much wider field, and one that cannot be dismissed so summarily. This rule applies to all combinations of consonant sounds that are, or may be, written by means of distinctive signs; but it applies imperfectly, for entire uniformity in the use of these secondary signs is unattainable. Still, it is not in vain to recognize the principle, **and apply the law wherever it can be done.**

a. Compounds of the **L** and **R**-series come under this law; and it is imperative in the use of all true initial compounds like *pl* in *play*, *pr* in *pray*, *fr* in *free*, &c. In final compounds the law does not demand the use of the compound sign, so its use here is merely for convenience.

b. The law of analogy demands also that all consonants that unite with a following *d* or *t*, as in the words *apt*, *act*, *art*, *and*, &c., represent such union by shortening the former of the two consonants. This principle is followed without any important exception; but the use of the half-length characters, where no such union of sounds takes place, is for convenience merely, and not demanded by the law of analogy.

c. The lengthened curves present another instance of the operation of this law; but it applies primarily only to cases in which a curved letter is followed by the sounds of *tr* or *dr* without an intermediate vowel, as in the words *after*, *enter*, *under*.

Rem. 1.— There is a conflict between the application of this law in the use of the half-lengths and the double-lengths, for in cases where *ter* and *der* are added to a consonant, the shortened form might be used, though not with the same degree of appropriateness.

After might be written *aft-er*, and *enter*, *ent-er;* but the true syllabication is *af-ter* and *en-ter*, which determines the mode of contraction.

REM. 2.— Other cases, however, occur in which the application of the true principles are not so obvious, as will be seen in the use of the different forms for *st* and *str*, as explained in sections 39, 40, and 48. The student is referred to these sections for further details in regard to the application of this law to half and double-length characters.

111. The operation of the laws of analogy may be traced throughout the entire system of word and phrase-signs. Whether a given principle extends through a larger or smaller class of words, it has a power to produce uniformity as far as its influence extends. But the action of one law is partially suspended by the action of another law in many cases. The termination *ward*, for instance, and the words *word* and *heard*, which express the *rd* by making the end of the stems of ⟋ and ⟋ heavy, have usurped so much territory from the action of the law which demands the expression of *rd* by means of a halved ⟋. The general rule could be followed in these cases, but, for the sake of briefer and more convenient word-forms, a new principle is introduced which, within a limited sphere, overrides the first or more general law.

SPEC.— Other examples of the operation of laws within a limited sphere will be noticed by the student. They need not be specified, as the object of these specifications is principally to call attention to principles which have already been detailed in connection with the rules for writing in previous chapters.

EUGRAPHY.

112. The term Eugraphy, from the Greek, *eu*, good or well, and *graphe*, writing, is used to designate that quality in the writing of Tachygraphy which gives to it grace and flexibility. It should not be confounded with the term caligraphy, which means beautiful writing, for eugraphy means not beautiful writing but the beauty or gracefulness of the writing.

SPEC.—The term eugraphy is applied not to the writing itself, but to a certain quality inherent in it, or to be cultivated in it. The term caligraphy, on the other hand, is the name of a species of writing instead of a quality pertaining to it.

Eugraphy may be further contrasted with cacography, which, perhaps, may be used to designate the badness or ungracefulness of writing, as eugraphy designates its grace and beauty. Cacography may, however, be also contrasted with caligraphy, and refer to bad writing in general, as caligraphy refers to good writing.

CHAPTER XI.

113. The principles of eugraphy apply to the *letters*, the *word-forms*, and the *phrase-signs*.

As applied to the letters, grace of form is secured by accuracy in direction, proportion, curvature, and shading.

SPEC.— The correct formation of the letters belongs to the elements of the science, and need not be discussed here. Yet, as some attention to the proper size and proportion of the letters is essential, both to beauty and facility of writing, the following suggestions may not be out of place.

a. Inclined, full-sized letters should be so proportioned in length as to fill the same space perpendicularly as the upright letters.

Ex.—| | \\ ⁄ ⁄ ⌒ ⌒ ⌒ ⌒.

b. The same principle will apply to the half-length, double, and treble-length characters. They each will fill one-half a space, or two or three spaces, as the case may be.

REM.— An earnest effort on the part of the writer to accustom himself to accuracy in this respect will be rewarded by an increased beauty in the writing. He should practice on each letter, contrasting its half-length, full and double-length forms with one another until he gains skill in making suitable distinctions.

114. The proper size of the letters for note-taking is one-eighth of an inch for ¡ and ¡ as the standard for the space occupied. The \\ ⌒ ⌒ &c. will be a little longer, and ⁄ ⌒ and ⌒ a little longer still than \\ &c.

Spec.—In making the standard of size for the note-taker one-eighth of an inch, it is not designed to urge this size upon all. Many persons will prefer to write larger characters for the sake of greater distinctness. Characters may be made of any size without interfering with the principles of eugraphy, provided the proper proportions are maintained. Yet, greater rapidity of writing can be secured in the use of small letters than larger ones.

115. As applied to words and phrases, the principles of eugraphy determine the comparative convenience of different outlines. Good outlines are those best adapted to speed and legibility: hence, the laws of eugraphy have reference, first, to the *requirements of speed*, and, second, to the *requirements of legibility*. These requirements coincide in some particulars, but not in all.

THE REQUIREMENTS OF SPEED.

116. The requirements of speed are based on the laws of motion, and relate to the *brevity*, *facileness*, and *lineality* of the outlines.

Spec. 1.—These terms are employed for want of better ones, although they poorly define the qualities indicated.

2. By facileness of outline is meant that quality in the

relation of the characters joined which renders transition from one to the other natural and easy. Some outlines may be written much more easily than others which contain the same number of strokes. Hence it is the province of the laws of eugraphy to point out the conditions under which the most facile outlines may be produced.

3. Lineality refers to the direction of the outline, which affects, in some measure, the speed with which it can be written.

117. *a.* The brevity of the outline will be generally determined by the principles of contraction. Yet some discretion may be used as to whether to employ a longer or shorter form for a word or phrase. Where brevity can be secured without sacrificing too much to obtain it, it is desirable; but the student should be cautioned against an undue regard for brief forms which are gained by a loss of flexibility or legibility.

b. All contractions demanded by the laws of analogy should be employed: those not demanded, but only permitted, should be submitted to the limitation of the other principles which enter into the formation of good word-forms.

118. The facileness of an outline depends upon, 1, *the nature of the angles made in joining* *its letters;* 2, the *homogeneousness of the curves that unite;* 3, the readiness with which the *word-forms* may be *joined into phrases.*

1.—THE NATURE OF THE ANGLES.

119. When the hand is in rapid motion, any change of direction must hinder the speed of the writer. If the first stroke glides into the second without an angle, the highest rate of speed can be secured. This gives a special value to forms, which are very numerous in Tachygraphy, like the following: ∪ ∩ ∩ ∩ ⊃ ⊃ ⌣ With these may be classed all letters that join without an angle, whether straight or curved. (See examples on pages 54, 55, and 56 of the Elements.)

Spec. 1.—With these may be classed also the so-called half-angles, such as

which in rapid writing run together without any angle.

2. All hooks, both initial and final, and the circles, add to the speed of the writer by bringing two letters into one stroke of the pen.

3. So, also, a circle between two full letters adds to the grace of the outline, except when it occurs on the back side of the curve.

120. When an angle must be formed, the more acute it is the more easily can it be made. Obtuse angles are especially objectionable, and should be avoided so far as possible. (See Elements, p. 54.)

Obtuse angles may be avoided in the Note-Taker's style in most cases, and better angles secured, as specified below.

SPEC. 1.—The use of vowel hooks and circles modifies obtuse angles wherever they can be used, as in ↶↷, ↳.

2. The use of half-length signs greatly lessens the number of bad angles. In most cases, where \ either precedes or follows —, the half-length letter absorbs it, as in ↳, ↳.

So, also, where — follows /, the / is halved, as in ↶. Other cases will be noticed in connection with other angles.

3. The skilful use of the variable signs will secure good angles in many cases where a careless use would produce bad angles. The variable letters are ⊂⊃⌒⌐⌒⌐/ /. Their proper use is discussed in the Elements, pp. 92, 93, and 94. See, also, the following section, where the proper use of the variable signs is determined in reference to the nature of the curves with which they unite.

2.—THE HOMOGENEOUSNESS OF THE CURVES.

121. *a.* Curves are homogeneous when they face the same way, or form any portion of a circle that may be made by tracing the circle in the same direction. Opposing curves are segments made by tracing the circle in opposite ways.

The curves (, ⌒, ⟍,), and ╱ (downward) are homogeneous; so are the curves (, ⟍, ⌣, ╱ (upward); but the curves in the first example are, each and all, opposed to the curves in the second example.

b. When an angle occurs between them, facing curves are made much more easily than opposing curves, for the pen traces a second curve in the same direction without an entire loss of motion; but when an opposing curve is made, the direction of the stroke must be reversed.

c. When opposing curves unite without an angle, they are made with perfect freedom.

SPEC. 1.—The following examples will sufficiently illustrate the nature of facing and opposing curves.

CHAPTER XI.

FACING CURVES.

OPPOSING CURVES.

2. When opposing curves lie in the same direction, and run into one another, they are more convenient than facing curves, as will be seen in the following examples:—

3. *a.* As a general rule, when a variable curve follows a curve of the same length, it may be turned so as either to unite without an angle or to face the same way as the curve to which it is joined. The union without an angle takes the precedence where it is equally convenient.

b. When curves of different lengths unite, those facing are always to be preferred, as an angle must in these cases always be formed.

122. *a.* These principles apply equally to vocal curves, and to the union of vocal and consonantal

curves. For these reasons ⌒ is struck upward after ⌒, and downward after ⌒. ⌒ (*El*) follows ⌒, and ⌒ (*La*) follows ⌒. For these reasons, we have the forms *La-and* for *land*, and *El-i-ent* for *lint*, and many others that will be noticed, where the direction of the letters ⌒, ⌒, ⌒, and ⌒ are varied on account of a preceding or following curve.

b. These principles apply also to the union of curves with straight lines or dashes. If a curved letter lies in the same general direction as the straight line, though an angle is needed, there is a continuous movement in the same direction favorable to speed; and if, added to this, the two may unite without an angle, the gain is still greater.

SPEC. 1.—The direction of the curves as controlled by the *dashes* is seen in the case of ⌒ in the word ⌒, and others. If the direction of the dash is reversed, the direction of the ⌒ will be reversed also.

2. Some exceptions to the principles given in this and preceding sections are unavoidable, for in many cases a curve occurs between two letters, with one or both of which it will unite with a greater or less degree of difficulty. If any of the letters are variable, as in most cases one or more of them will be, the difficulty can easily be reduced to a single bad angle; but even in case of variable letters, a change that aids the joining with a preceding letter may increase the difficulty of joining with the follow-

ing letter, and *vice versa.* Cases of this kind will afford scope for the ingenuity of the writer.

3. So in other ways one principle may influence or override the operation of another principle. Such details cannot be given here; but the teacher of the art is advised to add to the illustrations given, so as to adapt them to different classes of his pupils. Such instruction will bear good fruit in the increased beauty and facileness of the outlines.

3.—OUTLINES EASILY JOINED IN PHRASES.

123. Outlines that end in such a way as to be easily joined to a following word add greatly to the grace and rapidity of the writing. Such outlines may be secured in most cases by avoiding the use of final hooks, both vocal and consonantal.

SPEC. 1.—Vocal hooks are seldom used in the end of words in this style, and the use of consonant hooks is sufficiently limited in the instructions for their use. (See Chapter VIII.)

REM.—Those modes of contraction which encumber the ends of word-forms with signs that do not admit of connection with other words are so great a hinderance to phrase writing as to nearly neutralize their value as contractions. This is the case with the loops for *st* and *str* used in phonography. Forms of this kind have been purposely excluded from the Note-Taker. If they can be made of any use in a reporting style, it is only by carefully restraining them to certain words that do not occur in phrases very frequently.

THE LINEALITY OF OUTLINES.

124. Word-forms should have, so far as possible, a forward instead of a backward tendency. If the outline runs downward, or backward, away from the line of writing, it renders it unfit to form part of a phrase; and time is lost in bringing the pen back to the proper place for commencing the next word-form.

SPEC.—The student will see the application of this principle without extended illustration. The variable letters and the contractions may be so used as to favor linear word-forms. Such words, for instance, as *public, publication, aggregate, aggregation,* and others, may be relieved from running too far below the line by using the upward forms for) and / instead of the compounds (and \.

REM.—So much regard has been paid to this principle in the arrangement of the alphabet that it will be easy to secure good outlines by a little attention and care on the part of the writer. In any extreme case of difficulty, the word-form may be divided, as in the compound word *book-keeper.*

THE REQUIREMENTS OF LEGIBILITY.

125. The requirements of legibility presuppose, as a basis, a fair degree of accuracy of penmanship, and regard to the proper distinctions in the length and shading of the letters.

CHAPTER XI. 191

SPEC.—The student should be drilled on all the elements introduced into this style, contrasting half-length and full-length characters, full-length and double-length, double and treble-length, &c., till he can make the new distinctions as readily as those introduced into the first style.

126. The first special requirement of legibility as applied to word-forms is consistency of outline. When the reader has become accustomed to see a given word written in a given way, he reads it from memory, without looking through the characters to see what they spell. If the form be changed at random, he will read with slowness and uncertainty.

127. Another requisite of legibility is an observance of the laws of analogy. This will greatly aid the memory of forms, and the reader, becoming accustomed to see a given combination of sounds expressed in a given way, will read with certainty and ease.

SPEC. 1.—The operation of this principle is very subtile and far reaching. Suppose, for instance, that the writer omits the sign ⁄ uniformly in such words as *sound, bound, found,* and inserts the last stroke of the v as uniformly in *signed, bind, find,* and the u in *sand, band, fanned,* &c., the reader instinctively associates the sound of ⁄ with the open uncontracted and unvocalized forms ⌒—, ⌊—, ⌋—, and is led by the laws of analogy to expect the same sound before the uncontracted ⌣ in the words *ground, frowned, mound, crowned,* &c.

2. It will be observed that full, long vowels and diphthongs separate consonants, and that they generally accompany full and open outlines, while small and short vowels more frequently accompany contracted forms. This is especially true in regard to the use of the circle and the compounds of the L and R-series, and to some extent of the half-length signs.

128. A third thing essential to a legible style of writing is a proper distinction of words containing the same consonants. This has been so well provided for in the rules for the formation of outlines that it is only necessary here to call attention to the subject. If the words in question are of such meaning that they cannot be confounded, there is no danger; but if they are of like or opposite significations, there is need of a distinct difference in the word-forms.

Spec.—There is ample opportunity in this style for such difference of outline as may be necessary to legibility. When fully written, no word can be obscure or liable to be confounded with another; and where any form of contraction would reduce two or more words to the same form, the contraction should be applied only to the word of most frequent occurrence, leaving the others to be written more fully.

129. A proper use of vocalization may be

named as a fourth requisite of a legible style. A proper regard for brevity will lead the writer to omit all vowels that are not necessary; but it is unwise economy to add to the labor of reading to save a far less labor in writing.

SPEC. 1.—Vowels are necessary in some words containing only one consonant. Some of these are mentioned on pages 34 and 35; but the list may be increased. Besides these there are a larger number of words of two consonants, comprising nearly all uncommon words that may be written in full, as in the common style. The following will serve as specimens of the words alluded to in this specification: *bag, sag, ran, pan, cap, gap, map, rap, tap, mob, sob, jog, job, dame, cape, cake, wake, tall, gull,* &c.

2. In addition to these, many words of three or four consonants, with or without a contraction of consonant outline, may be vocalized.

Ex.—*Blab, slab, clod, plod, trod, shad, glad, clog, flog, grog, blank, flank, prank, brine, swine, twine, stripe, strip, strap, blame, flame, bloom, flume, broom, brim, trim, band, sand, bland, grand,* &c.

REM.—To these words in which the vocal sign is used for the sake of greater ease in reading should be added those given previously under the rules for the requirements of speed. (See sec. 120.)

3. The vocal v is frequently contracted before ⌣, as in the word ⌣, *bind;* and words ending in *ny* may be written in analogy with ⌣, *any,* by adding the tick. The last remark applies to such words as *bony, stony, cony, funny, honey, briny,* &c.

4. When two vocal sounds occur together, as in the words *aerial, pean, pious, science,* &c., one or both of the vowels should be written. The former, which is in most cases the accented vowel, is to be preferred when equally convenient.

5. Vocalization will be frequently necessary in the following cases:—

a. In writing proper names of persons and places.

b. In quotations from the Latin, Greek, German, French, and other foreign languages.

c. In technical terms used in the arts and sciences.

d. In all unusual words, or words used in an unusual connection, or in a peculiar sense.

Rem. 1.—Words generally considered technical or uncommon may be sufficiently familiar to some persons to be treated like ordinary words. The purpose of the writing, and the knowledge of the subject, will determine the amount of vocalization necessary to perspicuity. It is only necessary that the manuscript be easily read by the parties, and for the purposes, for which it was written.

2. The careless writing of bare skeletons of consonant letters, without any reference to their legibility, so common among amateurs in phonography, should be discouraged by the teacher.

130. A fifth requirement of legibility is *a proper regard to the relations of words in the sentence.*

Words that are used in familiar phrases, or in constructions that are familiar, become more easily legible from the connection in which they stand. But words that are isolated, or used in unusual connections, or in peculiar senses, demand more care in the writing to render them easily legible.

Spec. 1.—The power of position in a sentence to add to the legibility of word-forms is illustrated in nearly all the phrases given in Tables B, C, D, and E, and in Reading Lessons, pages 13, 14, and 15. Properly made phrase-signs will aid the reader by making the connection of the words ·more noticeable. The word *same*, for instance, becomes definite in the phrase ⌒, *the same*, since the word *some* is never preceded by the article *the*.

2. The joining of words, however, not associated in sense, would lessen rather than increase the ease of reading by intimating a connection between the words that did not exist.

3. Where words are isolated in construction, as in the following sentences, they need to be distinguishable in form.

Ex.—*But the fruit of the spirit is love, joy, peace, long-suffering, gentleness, goodness, faith, meekness, temperance. Can youth, or health, or strength, or honor, or pleasure satisfy the soul? I have seen the effects of love and hatred, joy and grief, hope and despair.*

Rem. 1.—Even in these cases, the reader is aided somewhat by the context, for he would not look for any evil affection or passion among the fruits of the spirit; and in the last example, the contrast suggests the contrasted word. So in nearly all cases the context will aid the reader to a greater or less extent; but he should not rely too much upon it, but take care that all isolated words be written clearly and definitely.

2. Uncommon words, and those of doubtful signification, with words from foreign languages, mentioned in the preceding section, cannot, from the nature of the case, be referred with safety to the

context for explanation, but must be legible independent of their connection.

3. Proper names that are mentioned among words needing vocalization may also be considered as isolated words, as they are not generally inferable from the sense of the passage in which they stand. Outlines chosen for autographs should be easily legible.

CONCLUSION.

131. When the student has gone through the preceding pages, and the writing and reading lessons which follow, he is advised to review the entire work, and to review it a second time, if necessary to its complete mastery. In no study will *thoroughness* bear better fruit. He should not rest satisfied, however, with the mastery of this little text-book, but apply the principles of the style in a larger variety of exercises, taken from works of value, by which he may add to his knowledge of the best literature while giving it a beautiful expression in the Note-Taker's style of Tachygraphy.

CHAPTER XI.

WRITING EXERCISE TWENTY-SECOND.

Form, formal, formalism, formalist, formality, formally, formation, formative, former, formerly.

Conform, conformable, conformably, conformation, conformer, conformist, conformity. Deform, deformation, deformer, deformity.

Inform, informal, informality, informant, information, informative, informer, informity, informous, inconformity, misform, misinform, misinformation, multiform.

Perform, performable, performance, performer. Reform, reformation, ref-ormation, reformative, reformatory, reformer, reformist. Retiform, scutiform. Transform, transformation, transformative, transforming. Uniform, uniformity, uniformly, uninformed, vermiform.

CONGRESSIONAL ORTHOEPY.—*A phonographic correspondent writing from Washington to the Cincinnati Commercial some years ago said,—*

"*During a rough and tumble debate on the confiscation bill yesterday, I paid a little attention to the manner in which certain words of common use in the English language were pronounced by different members. About twenty per cent of the representatives had something to say. The* Constitootion *was talked of freely, and great love for the instrument was expressed; eloquent appeals in behalf of the* institooshuns *of our country were made, and it was generally conceded they were very great indeed. Several inquiries were made by rural members as to* whar *certain authority was obtained from, and the reply generally was that if the inquirer would look in the right place, he would find it* thar. *It seemed to be a mooted question whether*

Congress had the right to con-fis-cate anything. It was asked if a dooplicate *copy of something or other could not be made, and a gentleman was referred to the Smithsonian* Institoot *for an* opportoonity *to get what he wanted. Life, liberty, and the* pursoot *of happiness were declared the* con-stitushunal *rights of everybody. The democrats thought the republicans were* revolootionary. *Eu-ro-pean precedents were quoted; and at home, here, we were referred to the fine States of* Ohia, Injiany, Noo York, *and* Missooruh. *These were all* prodoocing *States. Everybody was either a* com-*bat-ant or a* non- com-*bat-ant. The* Guver-ment *was assailed, and the* Gover-ment *was defended. The* Soopreme *Court was thought to be the highest law power in the land. Mr.* Sooard *was said to be the Secretary of State, and Mr.* Boochanan *the last President. The* abelitionists *were declared to be* fan-*atics. A great many men had been enlisted for three years, or* dooring *the war; but the* quoto *of some States was not full yet. Reference was made to* pro-vo marshals, *provost* marshals, *and the* Pro-vo Marshal General. *High eulogies were passed upon the people of certain* deestricks *because they had done their* dooty *in filling up the old* rigiments. *Men who didn't enlist were advised to get* substitoots. *Finally, somebody offered a* resolootion *that the House adjourn, and the members went home to sleep over their imperfect accentuation and pronunciation."*

A Universal Alphabet. — *We cannot but render homage to the efforts made by the powerful minds of those who have striven to reduce to a satisfactory unity the lamentable diversity of signs* (alphabets) *which have thrown such obstacles in the way of truth, and, either by fortuitous or designed resemblance, have so long retarded the progress of* the comparative study of languages, and their etymological affinity so important to their philosophical development, and, consequently, the knowledge of their real origin, as well as of the characters employed in writing,—fundamental principles which, in referring each language to its true source, would enable us to study each group of languages at the same time, and thus to obtain (if it were possible to devote sufficient time to each) an universal knowledge of languages.

To illustrate this proposition by an example, the study of the languages named Arabic, Hebrew, Samaratan, Ethiopic, Syriac, and Chaldean might, to a certain extent, be reduced to the study of only one, and a knowledge of the alphabets of each of the others, — alphabets founded, for the most part, upon circumstances which have wholly past away, but which, nevertheless, have given, and still continue to give, to each of the above-named languages an appearance of individuality which they do not in reality possess, but which will subsist until this appearance shall vanish, and all these languages be written with the same alphabet, whereby it would at once be apparent that they are really dialects of one and the same mother-language, — the Arabic. An able professor, who should occupy his scholars in this wide field of inquiry, explaining the rules of the mother-tongue, and the exceptions and peculiar character of its dialects, might teach six languages, or rather an entire family of languages at the same time.

An analogous idea, but of less easy execution, has been suggested, namely, the composition of an universal alphabet, or one embracing at least all the languages of Europe. —SYLVESTERE'S PALÆOGRAPHY.

WRITING EXERCISE TWENTY-THIRD.

No Excellence without Labor. — *The education, moral and intellectual, of every individual must be chiefly his own work. Rely upon it that the ancients were right, — Quisque suæ fortunæ faber. Both in morals and intellect we give their final shape to our own characters, and thus become emphatically the architects of our own fortunes. How else could it happen that young men who have had precisely the same opportunities should be continually presenting us with such different results, and rushing to such opposite destinies. Difference of talent will not solve it, because that difference very often is in favor of the disappointed candidate. You shall see issuing from the walls of the same college, — nay, sometimes from the bosom of the same family, — two young men of whom the one shall be admitted to be a genius of a high order, the other scarcely above the point of mediocrity. Yet, you shall see the genius sinking and perishing in poverty, obscurity, and wretchedness, while, on the other hand, you shall observe the mediocre plodding his slow and sure way up the hill of life, gaining steadfast footing at every step, and mounting at length to eminence and distinction, — an ornament to his family, a blessing to his country.*

And of this be assured, — I speak from observation a certain truth, — there is no excellence without great labor. It is the fiat of fate, from which no power of genius can ever absolve you. If genius be desirable at all, it is only of that great and magnanimous kind which, like the condor of South America, pitches from the summit of Chimborazo, above the clouds, and sustains herself at pleasure in that empyreal region with an energy rather invigorated than weakened by the effort. It is this capacity for high and long-continued exertion, this vigorous power of profound and searching investigation, this careering and wide-spreading comprehension of mind, and those long reaches of thought

> That pluck bright honor from the pale-faced moon,
> Or dive into the bottom of the deep,
> Where fathom line could never touch the ground,
> And drag up drowned honor by the locks.

This is the prowess, and these the hardy achievements, which are to enroll your names among the great men of the earth.—WIRT.

WRITING.—Whatever be the fate of this or that system, though every author perish without a name, yet the art of writing is not only commanding in its origin and history, but is beautiful in its graceful perfections, and imposing in its proper imagery. The true imagery of writing is culled then from the sublime and beautiful in nature; and here the mind cannot but contemplate its advent among the Hebrews with mingled emotions of veneration, awe, devotion, admiration, and pleasure. The summit of Sinai is clad with vivid lightnings, and rocked by the awful thunders of the Eternal, while amid the conflicting elements and blazonry of heaven's artillery the pen of the Law-giver is put forth to give his divine law, and the first tracings of this proud art to man. There he grouped in lessened lines the sun in his glory, and the moon in her unshorn majesty, the varied shore, the straits, the indentations, the sparkling islands, and culminating waves of the ocean. He blent the windings of the Euphrates and Jordan with the oaks of Bashan and the cedars of Lebanon; with the rainbow of the cloud he capped the tall pines of

Idumea, and mingled the rich shrubbery of Paradise with the spiral furs of Sidonia. Every dot was a star, and every cross [dash] a line of light from the eternal hills; and when the whole was finished, this wondrous art flamed out from the bosom of the rock, bearing the solemn and divine injunction of the moral law, as rules of action for all mankind. — KEY TO SPENCER'S PENMANSHIP.

WRITING EXERCISE TWENTY-FOURTH.

WRITING WELL. — *When a man would speak well, he must conceive clearly the ideas which he desires to express; and if he would write well, he must have distinctly impressed on his mind the characters which he means to exhibit. To illustrate the second essential of good writing, viz., power of execution, by the same analogy, however just and clear a man's conceptions may be, if his utterance be labored, slow, and timid, his discourse will be imperfect and unsatisfactory. In like manner, if the letters be well formed, but combined and arranged without ease or gracefulness, the writing will never be thought beautiful or pleasing. By long experience and observation in teaching, we are induced to believe that but a small proportion of minds are deficient in the faculty of apprehending proportionate forms, and happy blending of imagery, reflected through the medium of the eye. Such apprehension is generally developed with the greatest quickness, particularly when the judgment is assisted in its decisions by the active power and happy opportunity of comparison presented. Imagery, commended to our favorable notice and selection when young, by those we love, and* on whose judgment we depend, or left unforbidden to voluntary selection amid our school-boy scenes, when the young heart first begins to revel amid Nature's varied charms, and drink the smiles from friendship's sun-lit brow, makes a deep and lasting impression, which time and toil and age can scarcely mar, and never obliterate. Such is our nature. It is the poetry as well as the reality of our existence, embalming the scenery we loved in the innocent days of untried being.

Better is it for the noviciate in the art of writing to sit down alone with his materials and copy the moon in all her phases, borrow from the serpentinings of the brook that meanders at his feet, bring the Lombardy poplar to his aid, follow the curve of the pendant willow from tendril to stamen, and bind the whole with the undulating folds of the woodbine, and then call it chirography, than depend for a model of his hand on those miserable productions that, without form or comeliness, pain and perplex, and against the worship of which there is no command, either specified or implied. He would thus have more of nature, and therefore more of the true art of writing.

Thus, the proper images of writing being implanted in the mind, by having them early before the eye, are adopted by the judgment after comparison has done its labor and doubt has ceased.

The power to bring forth such imagery on paper is latent in the arm, forearm, hand, and fingers, and can only be developed by exercises that affect these auxiliary localities, and bring a fourfold power to act conjointly with ease and skill.

Without a free and unobstructed constant horizontal

movement from right to left through the whole line, the writing will be wanting in harmony of slope, ease, and truthfulness of combination.

But when all these movements are practiced fully and systematically, all the muscles from the shoulder downwards develop themselves rapidly, and power is gained over the pen to bring forth the adopted imagery of the mind in all the grace and elegance that spring from just proportions and easy execution.

Practice, to be sure, is indispensable in bringing to perfection any art, science, or profession.

The pupil must not expect to be able at once to execute what he fully comprehends. Patience and energy are required to attain a thorough and perfect command of hand. There is no royal road by which idleness and indifference may find their way to a goal which is only to be reached by diligent and well-directed application. The only process really short is such as is made so by commencing in a right manner from the outset, securing the advantage of the instructions of an experienced teacher till the object is accomplished. And when the object is accomplished, how beautiful and imposing are the specimens of art which the proficient is able to produce! The eye glances along the well-written page with as much pleasure as it rests on a beautiful grove when nature and art have unitedly tasked themselves to blend the greatest variety with the utmost symmetry.—SPENCER'S PENMANSHIP.

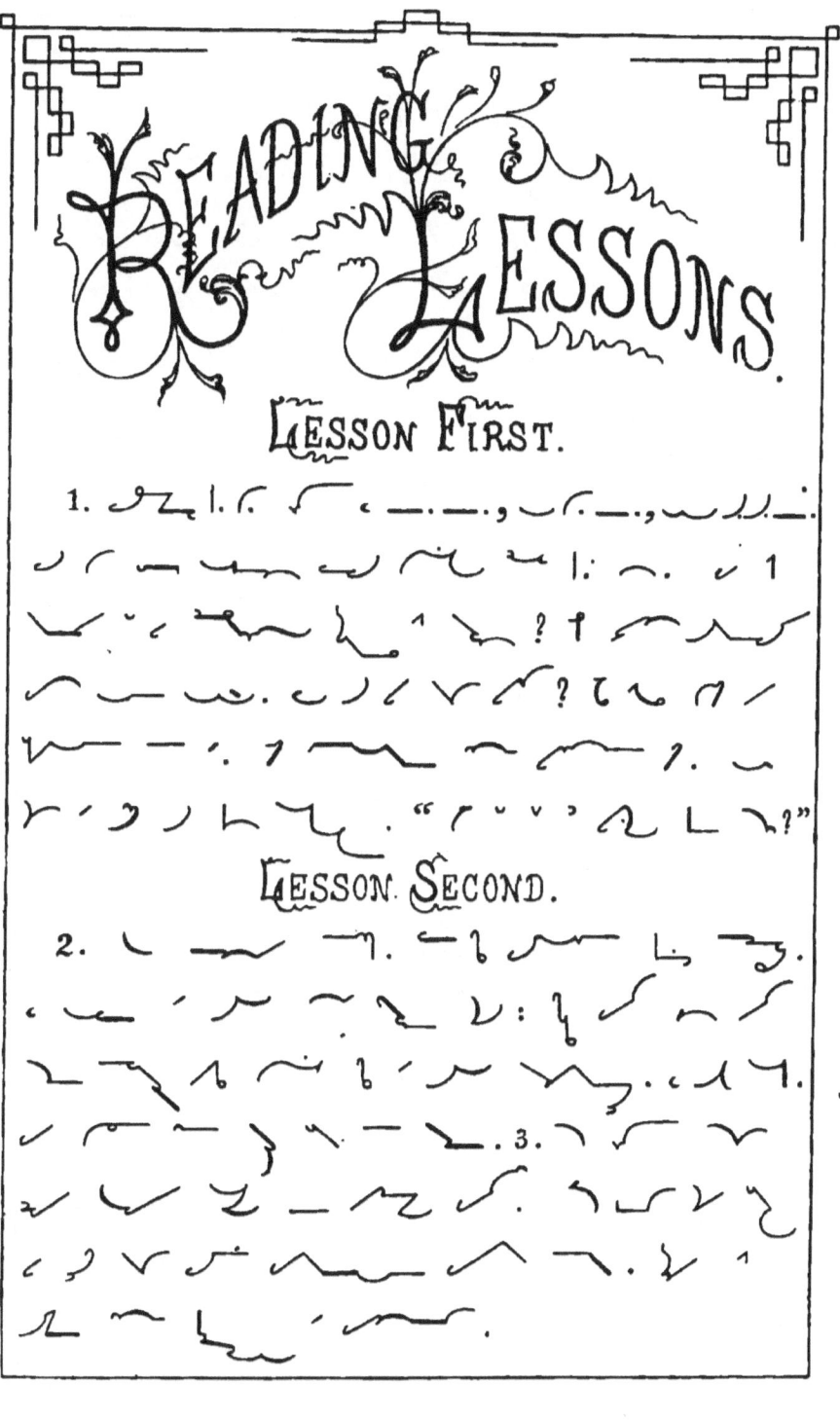

Lesson Third.

4. (See Sec. 12.)

Lesson Fourth.

8.

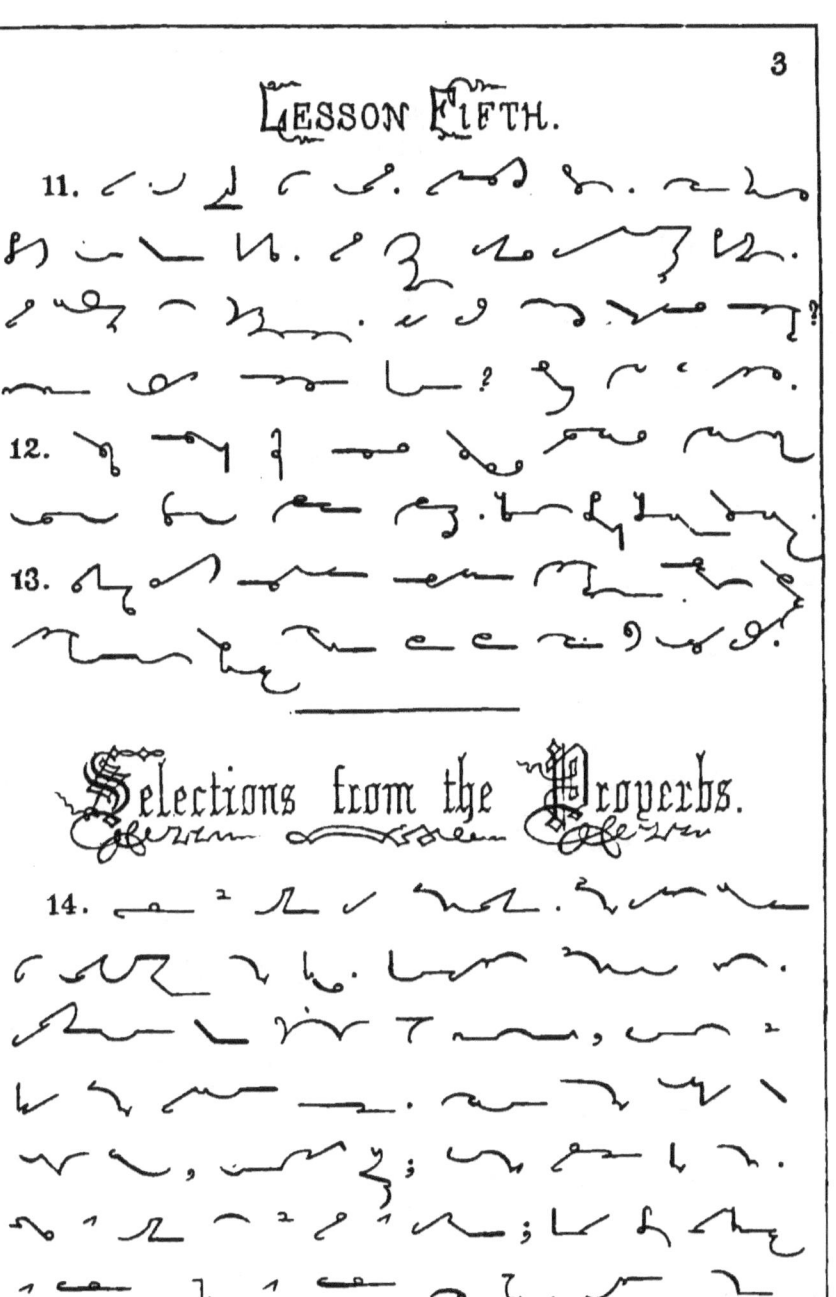

SELECTIONS.

SOLITUDE.

Hidden Joys.

Lesson Sixth.

15. [shorthand symbols]

16. [shorthand symbols]

17. [shorthand symbols]

18. a. [shorthand symbols]
b. [shorthand symbols] c. [shorthand symbols]
d. [shorthand symbols] e. [shorthand symbols]
f. [shorthand symbols] g. [shorthand symbols]

19. [shorthand symbols] 20. [shorthand symbols]

21. [shorthand symbols]

Miscellaneous

22. [shorthand symbols]

23. [shorthand symbols]

LESSON SEVENTH.

24. *a.* [shorthand] *b.* [shorthand]
c. [shorthand] *d.* [shorthand]
25. *a.* [shorthand] *b.* [shorthand]
26. *a.* [shorthand] *b.* [shorthand]
27. [shorthand]
28. *a.* [shorthand] *b.* [shorthand]
29. [shorthand]
30. *a.* [shorthand]
b. [shorthand]
31. [shorthand]
32. *a.* [shorthand]
b. [shorthand]
33. [shorthand]

LESSON EIGHTH.

34.
35.
36.
37.
38.
39.
40.
41.
42.
43.   44. a.
b.   45.
46.

LESSON NINTH.

47.

48.

49.

50.

51.

52.

53.   54.

55. a.

b.   c.

56.

SLANDER.

57.

Lesson Tenth.

58. [shorthand characters]

59. [shorthand characters] 60. [shorthand characters]

61. [shorthand characters]

62. [shorthand characters]

63. [shorthand characters]

64. a. [shorthand characters]
    b. [shorthand characters]

65. a. [shorthand characters]
    b. [shorthand characters]
    c. [shorthand characters]

66. a. [shorthand characters]
    b. [shorthand characters]
    c. [shorthand characters]

Nature.

67. [shorthand characters]

Lesson Eleventh.

68. *a.* [shorthand] . *b.* [shorthand] . 69. [shorthand] .

70. [shorthand] . 71. [shorthand] . 72. [shorthand] .

73. [shorthand] . 74. [shorthand] {[shorthand] 81} [shorthand] .

75. [shorthand] . 76. [shorthand] . 77. [shorthand] .

[shorthand]

78. [shorthand] ; [shorthand] . ([shorthand] 81) . [shorthand] , [shorthand] , [shorthand] , [shorthand] . [shorthand] .

Lesson Twelfth.

79. [shorthand] 80. [shorthand] 81. [shorthand] 82. [shorthand] 83. [shorthand] 84. [shorthand] 85. [shorthand] 86. [shorthand] 87. [shorthand] 88. [shorthand] 89. [shorthand] 90. [shorthand]

Lesson Thirteenth.

91. 92.
93. 94.
95. 96.
97. 98.
99.
100. 101.
102.
103.
104.

105.

LESSON FOURTEENTH.

106. *a.* [shorthand] *b.* [shorthand]
107. [shorthand]
108. [shorthand]
109. [shorthand]

Phrase Signs.

110. [shorthand]
111. *a.* [shorthand] *b.* [shorthand]
c. [shorthand] 112. [shorthand]
113. [shorthand]
114. [shorthand]
115. [shorthand] 116. [shorthand]
117. [shorthand] 118. [shorthand]

Anecdote. [shorthand]

Phrase Signs Continued.

119. [shorthand]. 120. [shorthand]. 121. [shorthand]. 122. *a.* [shorthand] *b.* [shorthand] 123. [shorthand].

124. *a.* [shorthand] *b.* [shorthand]. 125. [shorthand]. 126. [shorthand]. 127. [shorthand].

128. [shorthand]. 129. [shorthand]. 130. [shorthand].

131. *a.* [shorthand] *b.* [shorthand] *c.* [shorthand].

GENESIS. Chap. 1.

1. [shorthand]. 2. [shorthand]. 4. [shorthand]. 5. [shorthand].

Shortened Phrases Continued.

132. *a.* ... *b.* ... *c.* ...
d. ... . 133. ...
. 134. ...
. 135. ...
{or 3} ...
. 136. ...
. . .

Job. Chap. 1.

1. ...
2. ...
3. ...
4. ...
5. ...

THE ARMOR OF ERIC.

VOCABULARY.

The following word-forms, brought together and arranged alphabetically for greater convenience, are, mostly, illustrations of the principles scattered throughout the volume.

A

A, aye (forever).

abbreviate, brevity.

acceptance, accessible.

access, accession.

accident, accidental.

acclaim, accomplish.

accompany.

act, addition.

adjoin.

adjust.

advantage, advantages.

adverb, adverse.

advise, after.

agrarianism.

agree.

aimed, almighty.

already, although.

Alsace.

analysis.

ancestor.

anciently.

angel.

angelic.

anger.

angry.

another.

ant, &c.

anthropology.

any, anything.
apotheosis.
apprehensive.
apt, art.
article, as.
ask, assess.
astride.
auspicious, azure.
aye (yes).

B

back, baptism.
base, basket.
be, bee.
bean, because.
best, bestow.
bid, big, bill.
bind, binder.
bindery.

blow, bone, boon.
boned, bound.
bounty.
briskly, bristol.
bubble, burn.

C

Cæsar.
Cæsarea.
call, called.
card, cart.
case, cases.
cast, cession.
chair, chance.
chess, Cicero.
circumstance.
cisalpine.
clean, coalition.
coast.

VOCABULARY.

coaster.
command.
commend.
commander.
commingle.
commission, commissioner.
commit, common.
communion.
comply, compress.
concede.
concomitant.
condense.
conduce.
confession.
congratulation.
consent.
consider.
consists-ence.
console.
constitute.
contradict.

contravene.
coal, cool.
count, county.
counter.
culture, cultured.

D

danger.
dealt, deception.
dear, dense.
debts, doubts.
dell, dull.
dent, dental.
describe.
dissect, desert.
difficult-y.
discipline.
disclose.
discretion.

disorder.
dissuade.
distress.
do, done.
down, dun.

E

each, eat.
earns, earth.
edge, effort.
elder, elementary.
elements, else, less.
elsewhere.
emission.
encumbrance.
end, enter.
equal.
elision.
error, ever.

exclaim.
exercise.
exist, existence.
explain, express.
extra, cast.

F

fable, falsehood.
familiar, favor.
fetter, filter.
fiscal, fisher.
form, forward.
found.
founder.
foundry.
fragile.

VOCABULARY.

G

general, generally
gent, gentle.
gentleman-en.
get, got, gospel.
gradual, gradually
graduation.
grandeur.
Grecian.

H

half, hard, heard.
harden.
hardy.
hasty, hath.
he, head.
heavy, him.
himself, how.
however, howsoever.

hungry.
hunter.

I

I, eye, idea.
immortal.
impart, imply.
impel, impels.
impress, improve.
inbred, incline.
income.
index.
injure, initial.
insect, inspire.
instance.
institute.
instruction, insure.
intercommunicate
intercommunion.
into, intra, intro.

intransive.
intrepid.
intrigue.
introduce.
intrude.

K

knowledge.
know, no.

L

lagged, large.
language, long.
larger, latter.
length.
lessen, lesson.
letter, letters.
linger.
local, lofty.
longer.

M

magnanimous.
magnificent.
mainspring.
matter, mutter.
matters, mutters.
melt, moult.
member.
men, mention.
mental.
methodism.
mischief.
misinform.
misjudge.
misplace.
mission.
mistranslated.

VOCABULARY.

mock, mole.

move, muff.

N

national.

nationality.

nature, natural.

naturally.

necessary.

need, undo.

neighbor.

neither.

nevertheless.

nothing.

notwithstanding.

now.

number.

O! oh! owe.

object, objection.

objective, obscure.

obsequeous.

obstruct.

occasional, offspring.

ocean, omission.

office, offices.

on, own, one.

onward.

opportunity.

option, ourselves.

outrage.

over, overwhelm.

P

pannier, part.

particle, pebble.

VOCABULARY.

perceive, perhaps.

perish, pet.

pets, pent.

phonography.

physical, picture.

pictures, pleasure.

possess, possest.

post, poster.

practicable, practical.

practice, preacher.

precede, proceed.

press, presses.

principle, principles.

professional, professionally.

prophecy, prophecies.

proposition, propriety.

prosper, provisional.

Prussian.

pursue, pursued.

Q

qualify.

quench.

question.

R

races.

reason, received.

recess.

recognition.

recommence, recommend.

redemption.

regular.

VOCABULARY.

regularly.

remark.

remembrance.

render (to give account).

render (one who rends).

rendition.

rent, represent.

respect, rest.

restrain.

revision.

risen.

river.

rosin.

runs.

S

sad, sadder.

saddle, safe.

sanctification.

sanction, save.

says, screen.

secession.

section, seen.

self-admiring.

selfish, sell.

senses, sensual.

shackle, shall, shell.

shatter, shutter.

short, sit, seat.

sickly, signify.

significant.

sing, sung.

slaughter, smatter

smooth.

sober, social.	sustain.
society, soft.	system.
sole, soul.	
soon, sown.	**T**
sound.	tachygraphy (ta-kig).
south, spring.	teacher.
stir, strew, setter.	tell, tool, ten.
strayed.	tension.
stream.	test.
	than, that, thee.
subject, subjective	theism, then.
subsist, subscribe.	theist, them.
	these, they.
success, succession.	thing, this, though
successive, superb.	till, time.
sup, supped.	together, toward.
supper, sure.	transact.
suspicious.	transgress.

VOCABULARY.

transit.
translucent.
true, turn.

U

uncommon.
under.
undo, need.
unsatisfied.
unscrew.
unstrung.
up, us.
urgent, urgently.
use, useful.
utter, utters.

V

value.
vascular.
verb, vigil.

W

wellspring.
when, whensoever
wheresoever.
while, whim.
who, whole.
whosoever, whosesoever.
wholly.
will, willed.
withdraw.
word, ward.
wreathe.
wrongs.

Y

ye, you.

Z

zest.

TACHYGRAPHIC AND PHONETIC PUBLICATIONS.

THE ELEMENTS OF TACHYGRAPHY.

A Complete Treatise on the simplest style of the Art. The principles are illustrated by numerous examples of short-hand word-forms inserted in the text; by an extended series of exercises to be written by the student; and by reading lessons, beautifully engraved on copper. 120 pp. 12mo.

In cloth . . . . Price,	$1.75
Per dozen	16.80
In boards	1.50
Per dozen	14.40
Postage . . . . 10 cents a copy.	

☞ The Third Edition now on sale, is printed on paper of the first quality, in the neatest manner.

THE TACHYGRAPHIC ALPHABET.

With directions for its use, and reading Lesson with Key .	10
Per dozen	75

THE RAPID WRITER (*Quarterly*) for 1869, '70, and '71.

Volume 1, bound in cloth (postage paid)	$1.25
Rapid Writer and Philological Magazine for January and April, 1873	.25

THE NOTE TAKER.

A full Treatise on the Second Style of Tachygraphy, to follow the "Elements,"

Bound in cloth	$2.75

ADDRESS,

OTIS CLAPP & SON,
No. 3 Beacon Street, Boston.

D. KIMBALL, Box 398, Chicago, Ill.

NOTICES OF THE PRESS.

From the Conneaut (O.) Reporter.

For several months we hav compard it (Tachygraphy) with other systems, and ar satisfied that this is the best. It is more perfect, easier to lern, easier to read, and better adapted to general use.

From Rev. Peter Vogel, in the Christian Standard, Cincinnati, O.

It is becaus I kno whereof I affirm that I desire to speak. So long as men hav not found out the value and convenience of any given thing, it is no hardship for them to do without it. But who that has livd in our day of railroads, telegraphs, printing-preses, and kindred improovments, cu'd wish them banisht, or desire to hav livd in an age when these wer unknown? What these ar to former modes of travel, dispatching news, or disseminating information, is short-hand to the ordinary means of writing. . . . The phonography of Pitman, of Bath, Eng., surpast all previus systems. This system I studied, practist, and taught. Several years' experienc has forst the conviction upon me that as a corresponding style it is worthles, and for reporting purposes only the adept few wil ever use it. Tachygraphy, which is but a few years old, as a corresponding style, is more easily red than ordinary long-hand, and from three to four times as rapidly written. This I kno from experienc. As a reporting style it is adequate to a verbatim report, more easily lernd, and far more redily red, than any other system whatever. I hav studied the reporting style, but do not use it. The corresponding style servs all my purposes better. My advice to all literary men — preachers, lawyers, doctors, clerks — is, Study Tachygraphy.

From the American Farmer's Advocate, Jackson, Tenn.

THE ELEMENTS OF TACHYGRAPHY: CLOTH, $2. — We are indebted to the publishers for a copy of the abov. It is by far the most satisfactory system of "brief writing" we hav ever examind, and we hope the day is not far distant when it shal becom one of the studies of the common scool. To young men, to the students of our colleges, we unhesitatingly advise that they lern this system of rapid writing, and practice it until they becom expert. They wil never regret the three or four months' time devoted to it.

From the Daily Journal, Jacksonville, Ill.

We hav taken pains to examin into Mr. Lindsley's system, which he calls Tachygraphy, and can now speak of it in terms of the highest commendation. Possesing all the advantages of phonography, to which it bears som resemblance, Tachygraphy has so many markt excellences of its own, that it must be considerd far in advance of all other styles of short-hand. . . . The ease with which it can be lernd, written, and red; its simplicity, grace, and beauty, must commend it to all who ar anxius for something more economical of time and space than our present cumbersom long-hand.

From the Toledo (O.) Democrat.

The distinctiv feature of this system is continuity of pen-stroke by means of connectiv vowels. This principl is strongly illustrated in the superior rapidity of our long-hand writing, with its continuus stroke, over the ordinary Roman letter of print, requiring nearly every pen-stroke to be disconnected. ... We hav not time to go further into the subject at present. It is one in which teachers, clergymen, authors, and students, as wel as editors and reporters, hav a deep interest.

From the Detroit (O.) Commercial Advertiser.

We hav studied both these works (Graham's and Pitman's), and our experience is, that they ar so complicated and obscure, and withal so vast, that it seems like dedicating one's life to a wild-goose chase to attempt to lern it (them). True, these systems can be lernd; but then the person who expects to keep all these geometrical figures in his hed must not expect to hav anything else in his mind. After having gaind a knowledge of the art, it then requires years and years of practice befor you ar abl to use it with any degree of proficiency. Seeing these great difficultis, we had almost mentally resolvd to put our wits to work to invent a simpler and shorter method, when we herd of the new system, lately brought out, calld Tachygraphy. We hav examind it, and find it to be the most simpl system that we hav ever seen. And not only is it commendabl for its simplicity, but is actually interesting to the student. Every mark used in it is nicely calculated and laid out upon general principls. ... If we pretend to hav a reform in writing, we must hav a system that is plainly and easily comprehended. The times demand that som improovment on the old long-hand system should be made.

From the Reveille, (Publisht at Gen. Russel's Collegiate and Commercial Institute, New Haven, Ct.).

This system (Tachygraphy) has bin used in the scool during the past year, and has proovd easy of acquirement, and better adapted to general use than any previusly attempted. We recommend it to our readers.

From the New Bedford Evening Standard.

Those desirous of lerning a short method of writing wo'd do well to examin this system.

From the Carver (Ill.) Times.

The system of Mr. Lindsley is taught in first-class colleges, and is preferred by reporters and professional men above all others that hav bin introduced.

From the Peninsular Herald, Detroit.

The leading object of the RAPID WRITER is to introduce a simple and practicable system of Rapid Writing as the general and universal medium of communication. There is a pressing want in this direction.

From the Chicago Daily News.

In Tachygraphy the letters ar almost invariabl, and easily memorized. ... For verbatim reporting it is equal to Phonography, and for all other purposes far superior.

THE AMERICAN TACHYGRAPHIC ASSOCIATION.

To the Friends of Tachygraphy:

We hav frequent inquiries concerning the American Tachygraphic Association, and wish to say to those friends interested that it is an Association of such writers of Tachygraphy as desire to unite with others in their efforts to increase their knowledge of the art, or to aid in its introduction. Circles hav been formed for correspondence, which are found to blend instruction with amusement in a happy manner. Circulars explaining this mode of correspondence will be furnished on application, and those members desiring it will be introduced to circles.

The following extract from the Constitution gives the terms of admission:—

ART. III. SEC. 1. Any writer of Tachygraphy may become a member of this Association on application to any officer of the Association, and the payment to the Treasurer of the sum of one dollar.

SEC. 2. Children may be received with the consent of their parents or guardians at 15 years of age, but shall not be entitled to vote in the elections for officers of the Association until they reach the age of twenty-one years.

SEC. 3. Each member shall contribute to the funds of the Association, in proportion to his ability, a sum not less than twenty-five cents annually; and it shall be the duty of the President, with the aid and co-operation of the Corresponding Committees of the several districts, to organize and maintain circles for correspondence, to which all members who contribute one dollar or more yearly shall be admitted free.

SEC. 4. Any person eligible to membership may become a life member on the payment of twenty dollars at one time, or five dollars a year for five consecutive years, into the treasury of the Association. Life members shall be entitled to all the advantages of the Association, without further payment of dues or assessments.

SEC. 5. Persons not writers of Tachygraphy, but friendly to its interests, may be enrolled as Patrons on the payment of *ten* dollars. They shall not be eligible to office, nor subject to any dues or duties.

Note. Previous to 1873, all members were expected to pay $1 a year. It is hoped that the present arrangement will be more satisfactory to some who prefer to pay for the RAPID WRITER and for instruction separately, and that those who are able to do so will contribute liberally.

We hope that our friends, so far as they indorse these provisions, will endeavor to add to the membership of the Association, and to organize branch societies.

Tachygraphers willing to serve the Association as members of the Corresponding Committees are wanted to conduct circles in all parts of the country. Friends of the art, who are ready for the work, are requested to address the President. A Circular containing the districts to be represented, and the nature of the work, will be sent on application. Every possible aid and encouragement will be extended to members who conduct circles.

LET ALL TACHYGRAPHERS JOIN THE ASSOCIATION. "Come with us and we will do thee good!"

T. W. Hannum, Hartford, Conn., *Secretary.*
D. Kimball, Chicago, Ill., P. O. Box 398; *Treasurer.*
D. P Lindsley, Andover, Mass., *President.*

www.ingramcontent.com/pod-product-compliance
Lightning Source LLC
Chambersburg PA
CBHW031743230426
43669CB00007B/456